THE COMPLIMENTS OF
THE HOOVER LIBRARY ON WAR, REVOLUTION
AND PEACE
STANFORD UNIVERSITY, CALIFORNIA

THE PROBLEMS OF LASTING PEACE

THE PROBLEMS OF LASTING PEACE

BY

HERBERT HOOVER

AND

HUGH GIBSON

DOUBLEDAY, DORAN AND COMPANY, INC.

Garden City 1943 *New York*

PRINTED AT THE *Country Life Press,* GARDEN CITY, N. Y., U. S. A.

First printing, May 25, 1942
Second printing, June 15, 1942
Third printing, June 19, 1942
Fourth printing, June 25, 1942
Fifth printing, June 26, 1942
Sixth printing, July 24, 1942
Seventh printing, July 30, 1942
Eighth printing, September 15, 1942
Ninth printing, November 6, 1942
Tenth printing (revised edition), January 15, 1943

CL

Preface

THE AUTHORS wish to make acknowledgment to the number of persons to whom this manuscript has been submitted and from whom they have received most valuable suggestions.

They also wish to make acknowledgment to the research staff at the Stanford University Library on War, Revolution, and Peace, and to the Henry M. Robinson Research Fund of that library.

In order to make the book as convenient as possible for the reader, it has been divided into three parts.

Part I

Chapter I: Description of the seven dynamic forces which make for war and peace.

Chapters II to IV: The movement of these forces from the Renaissance until the first World War in 1914.

Part II

Chapters V to IX: The movement of these forces from the beginning of the first World War to the beginning of the second World War in 1939. Included is an analysis of the Treaty of Versailles, the League of Nations, and other peace efforts.

Part III

Chapters X to XIV: Conclusions as to the essential foundations of peace and the various plans and proposals to maintain the peace when the foundations are so laid.

Contents

Authors' Note

IN THIS EDITION we have revised several passages for greater clarity. For the convenience of the reader we have numbered our italicized conclusions—50 in number—and we have rewritten the last chapter to make clear that we are not proposing a prolonged armistice but on the contrary advocate eliminating the armistice period altogether through a quick provisional peace, with a cooling-off period for determination of economic reforms and the machinery for preserving lasting peace.

THE PROBLEMS OF LASTING PEACE

Introduction

OUR COUNTRY is now engaged in the greatest struggle of its existence. All Americans, regardless of their past views, are now united in a single purpose. That purpose is to achieve victory and thereafter build a world where we can hope to live in peace and security.

There lie before us two great campaigns. The first is the military campaign to defeat the enemy.

But the second and equally difficult undertaking is to win a lasting peace for the world. Military victory alone will not give us peace. That was proved in 1918. Victory, however essential, is chiefly important for the privilege it gives of shaping an era of peace for the world.

There must sometime be a cessation of hostilities, following which some method will be arrived at for making and preserving peace. It may be by mandates of the leading victors, or by a great conference, or by stages of settlement. For purposes of this discussion, we shall refer to these processes as the peace table.

And we must assume that if democracy is to live, these settlements will be submitted to the representatives of peoples in congresses or legislatures or parliaments, for ratification by each.

This essay is based upon victory and an American point of view. There are, however, reservations on any proposed American principles of peace that should not be forgotten.

In the first place, we must recognize that our allies in this war—Britain, Russia, China, and the others—will look upon the problems of peace through different eyes. We cannot know their conclusions at this stage. In the second place, we cannot foresee the kaleidoscopic shifts in the relation of nations which will probably take place during this war.

But whatever the fortunes of war may be, we feel that exploration of the past and the complexities of the future will demonstrate that it is essential that the principles and the methods of peace be threshed out and clarified in our own minds.

The men who gather at the peace table will have but a fleeting opportunity to make secure the foundations of lasting peace. Nations can blunder into war. They cannot blunder into peace. The wisdom and courage exercised in making the next peace will determine the fate of humanity for long years to come.

When the day of the armistice or any other end to military action comes, nations will be exhausted and many of them starving. The demobilization of armies, navies, and the workers in war industries will bring great economic and governmental problems to the victors as well as to the vanquished. Political stability cannot be founded, boundaries settled, armies demobilized, peaceful production started, hunger ended, reconstruction begun until peace is proclaimed. The whole world will be crying for haste. There will be little time then to think out the forces of lasting peace. That must begin now.

We were told in the last war: "Destroy the Kaiser first. Discuss peace afterwards." Today, again, it is "Hitler, Mussolini, and Tojo must be first destroyed; we cannot discuss peace until that is done."

We went to the peace conference in 1919 animated by the loftiest and most disinterested ideals, but we were totally unprepared for the specific problems that had to be met at the peace table. We secured neither peace, freedom, nor prosperity.

There must be just as much preparedness for peacemaking as there is for war. And in many ways the preparations for peace are a more difficult task. Preparedness for war deals mostly with tangibles—men, guns, ships, planes, money—and with tactics and strategy. Preparedness for peace deals largely with intangibles—the setting up of moral, intellectual, economic, and political forces over the whole world which will produce and hold peace.

And lasting peace cannot be made simply of lofty expressions of aims and ideals. Such ideals are necessary. We must have aims. But that is only the starting point of the job of making lasting peace. Any peace consists of a realistic definition of territorial, economic, political, military, and other settlements, with terms, methods, and machinery for carrying it out. The "aims" and "ideals" are not part of the binding words of a peace. They are only background to be expressed in undertakings of concrete character.

The difference between "aims" and peace treaties is the same difference as that between the Declaration of Independence and the Constitution of the United States. It takes little effort of the imagination to picture the results if, instead of elaborating a Constitution, the Founding Fathers and their descendants had endeavored to govern this country under the terms of the Declaration of Independence.

The vital question in the peace is how our aims and ideals are to be made to work. That is, by what means, what powers, what machinery, is peace to be made to prevail?

If we are to make a better job of the peace this time than last, it will be because intelligent public interest and discussion succeed in developing more ideas and better ideas. And it will be because of better understanding of the causes of failure in the past and the experience that can be drawn from mankind's many efforts in the prevention of war. And finally, if constructive plans for peace and justice could be developed, they might even help bring the war to an earlier victorious end. For today, great masses of people in the enemy countries are yearning for any peace which brings legitimate hope for the future.

There is no doubt that the tribulations of the world today are in large measure due to the acceptance of materialism and loss of spiritual standards. Without these developments there would have been no room for the growth of regimes based on brutality, the arbitrary use of force, and disregard of all the spiritual values which make life tolerable. If the authors do not labor this view it is because it is so staggeringly obvious that it can be taken for granted in an essay devoted to analysis of political problems.

However, for the sake of clarity it must be said that no political solutions, however realistic, will suffice to give us a peaceful world unless they are accompanied by a return to something better than a belief in material well-being—a return to faith in higher things.

This book is offered as a sort of preface to peace-making. It does not attempt to write the inevitable treaty of peace. But there are certain dynamic forces among men which make for peace and war. The world has had vast and bitter experience in peacemaking. This book seeks to draw from the experience of the past some principles, some methods of action, which allay those forces that make for war and strengthen those that make for peace. We have sought to distill some conclusions from the failures and successes of the past.

And there must be some organization, some machinery for the preservation of the peace when it is made. Again, the world has had experience and many experiments from which some guidance can be deduced.

There are indeed many plans now under discussion to preserve the peace. Some are Utopian. But there is no reason to scoff at Utopian ideas, for they stimulate thought, imagination, and discussion. Without dreamers, mankind might never have emerged from savagery. But again, there is great need to apply the tests of experience and to weigh such plans in the scales of the dynamic forces which will continue to work for peace or war.

Therefore, there are certain fundamentals upon which this essay is based:

First, that a satisfactory and durable peace must be founded on victory. Many of its essentials would crumble with compromise.

Second, that lasting peace can come only if the settlements take account realistically of the underlying dynamic forces in civilization that make for war and peace.

Third, that the new peace must provide for some organization, some machinery for international co-operation to preserve the peace once it has been made.

Fourth, that the American people must begin to think of the problems of peace. And they must think in a far larger frame than ever before.

Our hope is that we may here aid to stimulate American discussion and to clarify thinking. The authors' justification for venturing upon this subject is that both of them have had to deal actively with these problems for the past thirty years.

With a limited canvas for the portrayal of such a broad sweep of history as it bears upon war and peace, they have endeavored not to burden the reader's mind with detail that does not bear directly upon this major purpose.

We are in a gigantic war. Our first task is to win it. Having set our hand to the task, we cannot stop until lasting peace has been made. Only from a lasting peace can we hope to save our civilization.

To contribute to that end is the purpose of this book.

PART I

CHAPTER I

The Dynamic Forces Which Make for Peace and War

WE HAVE NOW had a generation of almost continuous wars, revolutions, and social and economic disorder, and the end is not yet. The world has seen such periods of explosion and degeneration before, separated by varying periods of more or less peace and human progress.

Boundary lines between periods of history are not always clear-cut, but they can be sketched with a broad brush.

If we scan the history of modern Western civilization, we can see the dim shapes of three great periods of new ideas and rising forces, each of which culminated in long world wars, tumults, and world disorder.

There have been three of these major widespread upheavals since the Renaissance. First was the Thirty Years' War, ending with the Peace of Westphalia in 1648; second, the forty years of war following the American and French revolutions, ending with the Congress of Vienna in 1815; and third, the world-wide wars beginning in 1914 and still raging.

In each of these periods, civilization took on new impulses, new forms, and new directions. Today we are probably in the presence of a third period of great change.

It is too easy to attribute our present wars to individuals or groups of individuals or even to perverse nations. It is easy to assume that lasting peace will come when these individuals or nations are punished as a flaming notice to future evildoers.

But great explosions in civilization do not have their origins in single men or a perverse nation. Such evil persons or peoples are themselves the product of deep-seated forces which must be stopped, allayed, or controlled if there is to be lasting peace. Those men or groups only light the match to a train of powder which has been laid over the years before.

Whatever may be done in making plans for the future or in writing the documents of peace will have no value unless account is taken of the evolving forces which have their birth in the years behind us. To gain some comprehension of these gigantic issues, we must reach into the dynamic forces that have been building this crisis—and must seek solutions that will ease the strains of the period to follow. And unless we are prepared to inquire objectively into and accept these forces as revealing the real problems of peacemaking, this war will be but the prelude to still another.

We must set aside our preconceived ideas on measures for making and keeping peace—that is, until we can establish whether they reach essential ills. The surgeon does not succeed in diagnosis by looking at the outside of his patient. He explores the action of the nervous system, the circulatory system, the digestive system, the cell structure, the pains, and the will to recovery in his patient. And this is a sick world—a very sick world.

The Seven Dynamic Forces

There are many of these dynamic forces that make for peace and war. They have been in operation unceasingly, though in varying degrees, ever since the dawn of recorded civilization. These forces can, for diagnosis, be separated into:

1. Ideologies
2. Economic pressures
3. Nationalism
4. Militarism
5. Imperialism
6. The complexes of fear, hate, and revenge
7. The will to peace

These forces are not arranged in order of their importance. That varies in different periods. They overlap and are interwoven into the whole fabric of civilization. Other students may prefer different divisions and different designations for these parts of world anatomy. We have reached the conclusion, however, that these divisions and separations most nearly represent not only these dominant world movements, but are historically the more conclusive basis, and they furnish a new approach in discussion of these problems.

The history of peace and war is largely a recitation of the operation of these forces and the failures of men to comprehend and control them. Much of it is mistakenly written into terms of personalities, both good and bad. Now is the time when the problems of this peace must be studied in far larger patterns than ever before.

Ideological Forces

The importance of religious faith, of social, economic, political, artistic, and scientific ideas, in shaping the form of the world and the making of its wars and peace is not to be estimated as less than that of other forces. Over the long range of history, they are the determining factors in civilization.

One thing is certain: that is, the ideas which involve human belief and faith contain a militant crusading spirit. Within them is inherent aggressiveness. Great and revolutionary ideas have within them at least a period where they are borne aloft by military action. Christianity, Mohammedanism, the Divine Right of Kings, the Protestant Reformation, and Liberalism have all in their time marched with the sword. Now, new ideologies—Communism, Fascism, and Nazism—are on the warpath. And ideological wars, whether religious or temporal, are more cruel and more bitter than were wars of mere conquest or exploitation. While the ideology of personal liberty is today less agressive than the ideologies of collectivism, yet it can rise to crusading heights.

Ideologies can also make for peace. For these nineteen centuries Christianity has been unique among religious faiths in its preaching of peace and compassion. Personal liberty and representative government as a political concept have also preached the gospel of peace. Both, at times, have sought to impose their beliefs with the sword. But their final purpose is peace. And as long as men have beliefs, they will strive to protect and expand them.

Economic Forces

While we have no faith in theories of complete economic determinism in history, yet it occupies a large place among these seven forces. Since men must have food and living, the striving for them creates eternal economic forces and pressures. Certainly, through the history of modern civilization, economic forces have played a large part. It was the wealth of the Indies which stimulated the great explorations and conquests of the fifteenth and sixteenth centuries. Pressures of overpopulation to find outlets for men and goods play a striking part on the world stage today. The cravings for security of supply of raw materials and places to sell surplus products have led to incessant friction, hate, fear, and war. Insistence that "trade follows the flag" has cost rivers of blood and untold sorrow. All these are part of the incentives to imperialism.

Whatever may have been the weight of economic pressures in creating the World War of 1914, the economic aftermaths of that war were among the primary causes of the collapse of the world into this second World War. War's disruption of economic life has been burned into the consciousness of nations, yet not so deeply as was hoped by some observers. But economic forces have also at times and under other circumstances acted as a restraint on war.

Nationalism

Nationalism has developed from the deepest of primitive instincts and emotional forces in mankind.

It gathers from a thousand springs of common race with

its common language, religion, folklore, traditions, literature, art, music, beliefs, habits, modes of expression, hates, fears, ideals, and tribal loyalties. It expresses itself in patriotism, which is itself built from the fundamentals of love of family, love of country, pride in racial accomplishments. Men fight for their hearths and their homes. They fight for their flag.

From all these racial instincts and mores rises the eternal yearning for independence from foreign subjection or domination. Thus, the subjection of races is one of the most potent of all causes of war. Nations are eternally striving for independence—self-determination. The oppressions which they suffer harden their souls and invigorate their resistance. All the thousands of years of human history are punctuated by wars of independence.

Who can even recite the repeated wars for independence of the Greeks, the Germans, the Spanish, the French, the Romans, and their successors, the Italians?

Nationalism will not be stilled by battle or defeat. It is fired to greater heat by every war and every peacemaking. A fiercer nationalism flares out of every defeat and every victory.

Victorious peoples who have marched to the defense of their homes and country to the stirring words of their national songs, who have followed their flags on the battlefield, who have sacrificed their sons and their wealth are little inclined to accept abrogation of their independence of action or of their sovereignty.

Nationalism can be both a cause of war or a bulwark of peace and progress. The values of nationalism cannot be ignored because of its secondary evils.

Where it is an impulse to strive for independence from oppression, for defense against aggression, it makes for war. But independence and spiritual unity, pride of country, constructive rivalry, the building of national cultures out of cohesive mores, the better conduct of government in areas of unity of thought and purpose bring more flowering of progress and the expansion of cultural institutions, scientific research, art, music, and literature. Nationalism in the best sense is a satisfaction, a fulfillment.

Extreme nationalism does have liabilities to peace and progress. As among individuals, there are ambitions in races for glory and for power of the race. Dignity, honor, and aggrandizement of his country is a satisfaction to the individual. To gain a place in the sun is an inspiring call.

Nationalism can readily expand into dangerous forms—greed in exploitation of the resources and foreign trade of other peoples and in aggression which quickly turns into imperialism.

There are about sixty separate nations in the world. And in the deep currents of human emotion, the primary interest of every citizen of them is his own country first and foremost.

Nationalism, with all its emotions, will continue as long as man inhabits this earth and will have to be embraced in any plan to preserve the peace.

Militarism

Man is a combative animal. He loves contest. He hates easily. He is an egoistic animal, and in the mass becomes more egoistic. His beliefs in superiority are quickly transformed into arrogance. And that is one of the stimulants of aggression.

The pomp and glory of war have an appeal to man. He loves adventure, and to great numbers of people war becomes a wholesale relief from the dull routines of life.

Common defense is an age-old instinct. It started with the defense of the family and spread to the tribe and finally to the nation. By reason of this need of defense, every nation must have some degree of military organization, even among the most peaceful peoples. The possession of armament, however, no matter how necessary, breeds suspicion, fear, counterarmament, and hate.

And out of military organization there often comes a military caste. Its hope of renown lies in war, not in peace. And its voice in government is more often for settlement of grievances by war than by the processes of peace.

The militarism we describe is an aggressive force. It always makes for war.

But military organization can have two quite different spirits. The one defense, the other aggression.

Like individuals, some peoples are naturally pacific and some, naturally aggressive. China has been outstandingly the most pacific of all nations. So pacific has she been that in 3,000 years she has been conquered and ruled by foreign dynasties in all but two comparatively short periods.

Moreover, there is in some races a definite aggressive warrior strain. It grows in an aggressive race to a glorification of war for war's sake. The "reinvigoration" of the race through war has long been preached in Germany, Italy, and Japan. The "warrior concept" is deeply rooted in Germany, particularly in Prussia. This may be because of the constant threat of invasion. On the other hand, it has been argued that the trouble with the Germans is that, unlike the French and the Britons, they were never conquered by the Romans and given the advantages of that form of education. Tacitus was eloquent on the subject of Germany nearly 2,000 years ago. The order of Teutonic Knights carried their thirteenth-century ideas with fire and sword. Their ideas of an aggressive military caste have come down through the centuries, with periodic modernizations, through Frederick the Great to Bismarck, with his "blood and iron," to Hitler with his "master race," his "guns instead of butter."

The same could be said of the Japanese. Their two feudal military clans—the Choshu and the Satsuma—are represented today in the control of the Army and Navy respectively.

Probably 80 per cent of the German and Japanese people are no more militaristic than any other. But, by their very docility, they are constantly overridden by the warrior groups.

And we must not overlook the Pied Pipers, consumed with ambition, who call their countrymen to glory and conquest. These men, seeking power on earth and a place in the eternity of history, are the apotheoses of militarism and aggression. They are the Alexander the Greats, the Ghengis Khans, the Julius Caesars, the Charlemagnes, the Gustavus Adolphuses, the Napoleons, the Kaiser Wilhelms, and the current exhibits.

Imperialism

Another of the larger forces moving in all history is imperialism. It may, for our purposes, be defined as the movement of races over their racial borders.

It is part cause, part effect. It springs from excessive nationalism, militarism, thirst for power, and economic pressures. They all feed upon one another. Old as the Chaldeans and as modern as this morning, its purpose has not changed, although its form has altered. At one time, part of the motivation of imperialism was dynastic or racial glory; at another, zeal to spread religious faith —for instance, Mohammedanism or Christianity. But in modern civilization its motivation has been chiefly economic.

Modern imperialism has developed into three varieties. of which one is justified by modern moral standards, the second may be justified, and the third has no justification in morals or hope of peace. The first variety is expansion of races into the settlement and development of areas mostly unpopulated; the second, into areas of uncivilized races incapable of self-government; the third, sheer conquest of civilized races. The last two have always embodied one purpose—that is, to secure superior living by exploiting other races and their resources.

Whether its impelling force be glory, prestige, spread of religion, ideology, development of backward races, or exploitation of labor and resources, imperialism is not essentially an appendage of the Divine Right of Kings or the attribute of dictators. Democracies have been no less imperialistic than kings, emperors, or dictators. Rome was imperialistic before the Emperor was invented. Britain and France and the United States have expanded steadily. But wherever imperialism has been successful over long periods, it has always rested upon class government.

There can be no doubt that domination and exploitation of other races is one of the eternal causes of war. We know of no case where it has made for durable peace. Even in the phase of expansion over backward races or into open spaces, the rivalries between imperialisms have made for war. In the spread of civilization, it has compensations. But as a method of advancing peace, it cannot be given a great deal of credit. Much can be said for a satiated empire like Britain, which has arrived at a point where it becomes a stabilizing force. More especially that Empire, being liberal in instinct, makes for representative government among its components.

But imperialism as a theory of maintaining peace in the modern world has the disturbing consequences of setting up a dozen rival forms of Pax Romana to fight one another.

Imperialism has been present at every peacemaking, and it will be there next time.

The Forces of Fear, Hate, and Revenge

Fear, hate, and revenge play a large part in the causes of war. The greatest of these is fear. Hate and revenge often spring from it. Fear of invasion, fear of starvation by blockade in war, fear of economic disadvantage; age-old hates from wrong, from rivalries, from oppression; yearnings for revenge for past wrongs and defeats—all press toward violence.

These great forces of violence lie deep in the recesses of racial consciousness and racial experience. These emotions are the inheritance from all previous wars. Wrongs live for centuries in the minds of the people. There are traditional age-old hates between nations which are burned into their souls. From these emotions, wars have bred new wars. They have seldom settled anything. Fear of stronger races by their weaker neighbors born of invasions and defeat keeps them in constant sacrifice for the burdens of defense.

It keeps them in constant agitation, seeking diplomatic action, seeking support and military alliances. And the humiliations and privations of defeat and punishment create an undying demand for revenge.

The defeated are always humiliated. They are always impoverished. Either in reality or belief, the national pride, the national hopes, the national economy, or the national dignity of the vanquished have suffered. No nation ever recognizes or admits that it is wrong. No leader of that nation would dare suggest such a thing. Hate lives on, and it becomes entrenched in the mores of a people.

These emotions are eternal inheritances and causes of war. They, too, will sit at every peace table.

The Will to Peace

Against all the forces which make for war stands the will to peace. Ever in the background of men's minds is the infinite suffering of war. It kills or maims the best of the race. It brings the deepest of griefs to every home. It brings poverty and moral degeneration. It brings these poignant ills to victor and vanquished alike.

The Sermon on the Mount launched the transcendent concept of compassion, of peace and good will among men as a fundamental of the Christian faith. "Blessed are the peacemakers, for they shall be called the children of God" epitomizes man's noblest hope. And despite all his violation of these spiritual concepts, man has received from them an undying inspiration to strive for peace.

The search over centuries by men of good will for methods of lasting peace testifies to the yearning of peoples for relief from the world's greatest scourge. The multitude of peace treaties, the establishment of embassies and legations, the Holy Alliance, the Concert of Europe, the balance of power, the Hague Tribunal, the processes of settlement of controversy by negotiation, by mediation, by arbitration, the League of Nations, and the World Court are all exhibits of the impelling will to peace.

And indeed, the spiritual concepts of peace have brought it to pass that every war must be justified by its leaders as a war of defense and for the one purpose of securing peace. And the end of every war is received with joy and the ringing of church bells.

Conclusion

These seven dynamic forces—ideologies; economic pressures; nationalism; imperialism; militarism; fear, with its consequences, hate and revenge; and the will to peace—have largely shaped the history of the world. The shapes have been different in different periods of history, for these forces have varied in their relative potency. They will continue to shape the world; they will haunt the halls of the next peacemaking. It will not be a new world after this war. It will be a different world.

We must not overlook the part which individuals may play. When great crises arise from these forces, they must be dealt with by statesmen. No student of history can ignore the part such men have played in the crises of war and peace. When these great pressures are met successfully, it means peace; when there is failure, it means war or the seeds of war. The leaders in times of crisis may be men of ability, character, courage, and vision. Or they may be men of ignorance, incompetence, consuming vanity, egotism, ambition, or corruption. They may be Utopian dreamers. They may be a mixture of these characteristics, good and bad. We agree that they have an immense responsibility. But the character of men should not obscure the fact that the fundamental approach to the problems of peace and war lies in recognition of the great forces in motion. The influence of statesmanship upon these forces holds a secondary place.

Whatever the weight of the individual may be, we are confronted with these dynamic forces and total world disorder now. And therefore, some recognition of these forces, some exploration of their impact upon peace and war in the past, some estimate of how they can be controlled in the future are vital if we are to be prepared to overcome the evil and promote the good by peacemaking.

CHAPTER II

Former Great Crises in the Modern World

IT IS OUR PURPOSE to explore the movement of these seven dynamic forces in the present world upheaval and their relationship to future peace. For the problems of today, the largest importance lies in the period of 165 years since the American and French revolutions. We shall in subsequent chapters divide that discussion into the periods:

From the American and French revolutions during 140 years to the World War of 1914.

During the four years of the first World War, from 1914 to 1918.

During the Armistice and the peace conference of 1919.

During the twenty years from 1919 to the resumption of World War in 1939.

As we have said, boundary lines between periods of history are not precise, but they can be sketched with a broad brush.

Our present gigantic crisis has sources in all history. And before we discuss the movement of forces in the periods named above, we will in this chapter shortly review some of the previous upheavals of modern Western civilizations. They have a bearing upon the problem as has also the early development of ideas for the preservation of peace.

The First Modern Crisis

The first of these great crises may be said to have been born in the rise of cultural, political, and religious ideas which gave impulse to the Renaissance and the Protestant Reformation and marked the emergence from the Dark Ages.

The period of gestation of these revolution-bearing ideas extended from the middle of the fifteenth to the middle of the sixteenth century. In this period, the movement of ideas and the spread of conflict was greatly stimulated by the expansion of the art of printing. The method of warfare was transformed by greater perfection in firearms. And in this time world-wide free economic enterprise found its beginnings.

In this period also can be seen the beginnings of a shift in civilization from the dominantly religious and spiritual basis prior to the Renaissance, to the dominantly materialistic basis that was to follow.

From all these enlivening ferments came the great era of world exploration which added the Western Hemisphere to European concerns, the discovery of the sea routes to the Indian Ocean via the Cape of Good Hope, and to the Pacific via Cape Horn.

Nationalism, imperialism, and militarism were not

idle. And wars which had been chiefly religious and dynastic in character gave way to wars for conquest.

Finally, the strains in these forces rose to the Thirty Years' War, involving every nation in Europe. One third of the population of Europe is said to have died in that war and from famine and pestilence after the Treaty of Westphalia in 1648.

The Second Modern Crisis

During the next 130 years, from the Thirty Years' War to the American Revolution, many different religious, dynastic, and imperialistic wars raged over parts of Europe. They did not, however, become universal in character. Some countries remained isolated from war in long-enough intervals for cultural ideas and economic life to make progress, stimulated by colonial expansion and overseas trade.

But in the latter part of this period—the end of the eighteenth century—a new world crisis was fermenting. Gradually, nearly 2,000 years after free Greece and early Rome, there came a resurgence of the idea of the rights of the individual man. This resurgence of the freedom of men is amply indicated at Runnymede, in the Puritan Revolution, in the Declaration of Rights, in the emigrations to America, in the work of the French Encyclopedists. But it is not our purpose to discuss its growth in detail.

Along with these dynamic ideas were again economic and nationalistic pressures, imperial and militaristic growths, and a generous seasoning of fear, hate, and revenge. The conflict and pressures of these forces finally began to explode in the American and French revolutions.

There followed forty years of wars, revolution, and

disorder involving, at one time or another, all the Western World. The outstanding militaristic figure of this period was Napoleon. Peace was made at the Congress of Vienna in 1815.

The century which followed was marked by growing recognition of the rights of the individual man and the rapid expansion of representative government, by the Industrial Revolution, by vast expansion in science and invention and the arts. Within this period there were great pressures from the seven dynamic forces which, with the failures of statesmanship in attempting to allay them, led to the explosion of 1914.

Early Efforts to Preserve Peace

During all the history of man there have been strivings to find methods for preserving peace. In our discussions nowadays, we are inclined to assume that our own generation is the first to see the light and that we have brought to bear on the age-old problems of war and peace a new vision and a new intelligence. A study of the past is always a wholesome corrective for this assumption of superiority.

From time immemorial, nations have marked the end of their wars by the signature of treaties of "perpetual peace" and solemnly promised its continuance. We are, however, at this point interested not in promises, but only in methods for preserving peace. Aside from the ancient Chinese proposals of arbitration and some settlement of controversies among the early Greek states, the first workable scheme for the preservation of peace was the Pax Romana.

In giving a short account of these early movements we have not attempted exhaustive treatment. We have done no more than discuss those which made a special impression upon their times and gave some lasting impulse. There were thousands of other writings and millions of preachers of peace and good will. And always the greatest of all contributions to the building of moral and spiritual foundation of peace began with the Sermon on the Mount. These teachings of Christ have thundered down over these 1900 years.

Governmental action to preserve peace began perhaps with that first unknown treaty at the end of some now-forgotten war which bore the startling designation of a "treaty of perpetual peace."

Pax Romana

The Pax Romana is proverbial and the model of various later systems which have not always admitted the resemblance.

Its short description would be the enforcement of peace by a dominant military power, with recognition of the rights of the defeated. The analogy with some modern proposals is more than superficial.

With the triumph of the Roman Empire at the beginning of the Christian era came a period of peace which lasted for more than three centuries. That is to say, there was peace within the Empire, although there was constant fighting on its frontiers.

It was possible to keep the peace during this period because Rome alone had a high degree of military and administrative efficiency and, on the other hand, was threatened by no redoubtable neighbor. For the most part, her immediate neighbors were barbarians. These could be dealt with by the use of police forces. Parthia, the only serious rival, was far away and hardly offered a threat of invasion.

The maintenance of peace was not an end in itself. Rome was like the Britain of our day in that she was dependent on food from overseas. To keep the sea lanes open, it was necessary to suppress piracy and other naval Powers on the high seas. Under this regime of freedom of the seas, trade with India was developed in order to avoid payment of the ruinous Parthian tolls on the overland route.

The strength of the Empire within its borders was not due entirely to fear inspired by the Roman Eagles, but perhaps more by developments in the outlying regions of the Empire: local government, roads, aqueducts, the fostering and protection of agriculture, and, above all, the benefits of Roman law.

Like all methods for maintaining the peace by force, the Pax Romana came to a disastrous end. It came to an end from forces within the Empire. Military attacks from beyond the frontiers were only contributing factors. The stamina of the peoples of Italy and Greece was sapped by the spread of malaria, and the peasantry was wiped out by the growth of slavery and the development of huge landed properties. Finally, in desperation, a sort of "managed economy" was introduced by Diocletian. The growth of centralized power and dependence on the Legions for order and protection left no fund of local strength or of public spirit for defense upon which to fall back.

Hitler's "New Order" is often compared to the Pax Romana, but there is an essential difference. The Pax Romana was established as the only alternative to barbarian violence and chaos, from which it emerged. Hitler has imposed and substituted his system by force after destroying an established regime of law and order.

Role of the Papacy

In a brief study of this sort we cannot hope even to outline the important role of the Papacy in the struggle for peace. A separate volume could be profitably devoted to this phase of the Church's activities during nearly two thousand years.

In an age of unbridled cruelty the Church took the first steps toward regulation and restraint of warfare. A notable instance of this was the "Peace of God"—a tenth-century attempt to do away with private warfare. This was an early effort to compel those accustomed to bear arms to agree not to use them and to submit their conflicts to the judgment of tribunals. These judgments were sanctioned by spiritual penalties. The scheme was not successful partly because the nobles were unwilling to forego the use of arms or to accept the decisions of the tribunals. The Peace of God was later (in the eleventh century) supplemented by the Truce of God, designed to regulate what could not be suppressed. It prescribed that there should be no private warfare during certain seasons and on certain days. The seasons included the time from Advent to Epiphany and from Septuagesima to one week after Pentecost. Throughout the rest of the year hostilities were forbidden from sunset on Wednesday until Monday morning and on all saints' days. By the end of the eleventh century private warfare was forbidden on all but some eighty days in the year. Sometimes the national sovereign supported the decrees of the Church, which thus became law of the land.

During many centuries the temporal sovereigns recognized the primacy of the Pope, not only in spiritual matters, but also in matters of government, war, and peace as well. Throughout this period the Church exercised a powerful restraining influence rendered doubly necessary by the standards of the times. Some of the solutions were of a character that could be imposed by a clearly recognized authority, as when Pope Alexander VI drew a line on the map and divided the overseas world between the great colonizing powers, Spain and Portugal. The penalties were of a spiritual character, culminating in the dread sanction of excommunication.

The influence of the Church was effective in averting warfare and contributed materially to the growth of higher standards of international conduct.

The Protestant Reformation brought a cleavage in authority, but in spite of this the voice of successive Popes has been raised in the cause of peace. The loss of temporal power in no sense lessened the moral authority of the Papacy, and the pronouncements of the present Pontiff command the respect of Catholic and non-Catholic alike.

The Protestant churches have been no less vigorous in teaching the moral foundations of peace. In our own time the organizations of Protestant churches have devoted systematic effort to this subject and have made a precious contribution to stimulating thought and awakening our people to the need for grappling with the problems of peace.

The Development of Peace Plans

From the Middle Ages down to the second great crisis, culminating in the explosions of the American and French revolutions, there was a wealth of plans for averting war and keeping the peace. Allowing for the differing conditions, they are strikingly like the plans of our own day. There are plans for a League of Nations. There are plans for federations. We find supergovernment and an international force to impose its rulings, collective security, mutual assistance, sanctions against an aggressor—even the radical idea of applying undiluted Christian morality to international affairs.

The Proposals of Gerohus

Gerohus of Regensburg, about the time of the Third Crusade (1190), advanced a plan for abolishing war. Gerohus saw the problem in simple terms. In his view, it would suffice for the Pope to forbid all war—an early version of the outlawry of war. He proposed that once this was done, all conflicts between princes should be referred to Rome for decision—here we have compulsory arbitration. And finally, any prince rejecting the arbitral award should be excommunicated and deposed—sanctions with a vengeance.

The Plan of Pierre Dubois

A plan for a League of Nations appeared in the fourteenth century. In a document entitled *On the Recovery of the Holy Land,* Pierre Dubois of Normandy, an adviser of Philip the Fair, advocated a federation of Christian sovereign states. There was to be a Council of the Nations to arbitrate all quarrels. There was a catch in this scheme, however, as in many later ones, in that it was prescribed that France should be dominant in Europe and that the Council of the Nations should concentrate its efforts on subjugation of the infidel.

The Proposals of Dante

Even Dante, in his *De Monarchia,* tried his hand at designing a brave new world. He was primarily concerned with arguing the case for the Emperor against the Pope. The Empire had existed, he said, before the Church, and as Aeneas was the ancestor of the Romans, they were of a superior race and thus qualified to govern lesser breeds. Already, in the fourteenth century, Dante had his version of Aryan superiority.

In discussing controversial matters in his dangerous times, it was prudent to seek safety in allegory, and Dante's argument is sometimes cryptic in the extreme. But he did put forward the idea that human happiness must come from the reign of law. He did not advocate the supremacy of one state over another, but the supremacy of law over all, so that national passions might be held in check—in other words, international law for arbitration of disputes. There would be a supreme power under "the ideal prince" to give needed guidance. He desired that Italy should be "an angel of light among the nations," but he did not desire her to be dominant.

Rather, she was to become a member of a world state guided by a Supreme Court of Justice.

The Great Design of Henry of Navarre

Henry of Navarre (1553–1610) and his adviser, the Duc de Sully, produced a more specific and detailed plan, the Great Design.

According to Sully the plan seems to have arisen from Henry's conviction that the humiliation of the House of Austria was essential to his own safety. But after this was achieved it was desirable to set up a regime in Europe that would keep the peace.

Austria having been destroyed, Europe was to be re-divided among fifteen Powers in such equal portions as would prevent any future uneven balance of power—a drastic and original method.

Having redrawn the frontiers of Europe, Henry set up —on paper—his League of Nations. The fifteen Powers were to be represented in a Great Council, whose members would be subject to re-election every three years. The expenses of the Council were to be paid by proportional contributions from the member states. It would be the duty of the Great Council to settle disputes of all sorts among the states and to deal with current affairs.

Thus far, Henry kept closely to the lines of the future League of Nations. But he further proposed an international army and navy to enforce the decisions of the Great Council.

While the Great Design was to do away with war among the fifteen member states, yet it was not so radical as to forbid aggression against outsiders. Territories conquered in this way would be formed into new kingdoms, which would be given to princes put out of work by the reorganization of Europe—and these new kingdoms would be admitted to the Christian Republic.

It was prescribed that the Council should adopt "to the contentment of all parties" such laws as were calculated to cement the union of all states and to maintain order, freedom of trade, etc. And it was prescribed that the Council should undertake reforms which would from time to time be necessary. This was a wise and farsighted regulation by which Henry of Navarre proposed the peaceful revision of treaties.

Henry's plan was never put into operation, although Sully tells us it was on the eve of being tried "when it pleased God to call him too soon for the happiness of the world." But it has been a mine of precedent and ideas for every substantial plan for international government. It is the first balanced plan of federal partnership among sovereign states, with machinery for the peaceful settlement of international disputes and an international force to apply sanctions.

The Proposals of Emeric Crucé

Emeric Crucé produced his *Nouveau Cynée* some twenty years after the Grand Design of Henry of Navarre. He went further in two particulars. He advocated that membership in the League of States should be open to non-Christian as well as Christian states—which thus opened the door to world federation. He further proposed that war should be done away with by the adoption of a comprehensive system of arbitration.

The Plan of William Penn

William Penn advanced in his *Essay towards the Present and Future Peace of Europe* (1693) a scheme for the future organizing of the world which he hoped would create tremendous benefits. By stopping war, he hoped to avoid bloodshed, save money, strengthen Christianity's reputation, increase trade and commerce—and make it possible for princes to marry for love, not power. A permanent International Tribunal was to be set up by the sovereigns of Europe, consisting of ninety representatives, chosen by a system of proportional representation, meeting every year to discuss and settle all international differences not settled by diplomatic means. Decisions were to be made by ballot, with a minimum majority of three quarters of the votes. Business was to be done in Latin or French, records to be circulated to each sovereign.

There is a general impression that Penn avoided the question of the use of force to compel a state to abide by an arbitral award. It is assumed that it would have run counter to his faith to provide sanctions. As a matter of fact, he recognized the need for sanctions in clearly providing for common action against an offender in the following terms:

> If any of the sovereignties that constitute these imperial states shall refuse to submit their claim or pretensions to them, or to abide or perform the judgment thereof, and seek remedy by arms, or delay their compliance beyond the time prefixed in their resolutions, all the other sovereignties, united as one strength, shall compel the submission and performance of the sentence, with damages to the suffering party, and charges to the sovereignties that obliged their submission.

In other words, he prescribed common action involving the use of sanctions of more violent order than those of the League of Nations.

The Plan of Saint-Pierre

Charles Irénée Castel, Abbé de Saint-Pierre's *Project for Settling Perpetual Peace in Europe* (1713) was prompted by the sordid bargaining that went on at the peace negotiations at Utrecht at the end of the War of the Spanish Succession. It shows the inspiration of Henry of Navarre.

Saint-Pierre proposed: a League of Sovereign States in a permanent Congress of Representatives; a code of Articles of Commerce; arbitration of disputes by a permanent Senate; combined military sanctions against a rebellious state; reduction of peacetime armies in all states to 6,000 men; weights, measures, and coinage to be standardized throughout Europe; creation of a similar self-contained Asiatic League.

The Plan of Jean Jacques Rousseau

Jean Jacques Rousseau's *Judgment on a Plan for Perpetual Peace* (1761) sought to improve on Saint-Pierre's plan by guaranteeing the existing *status quo* and rendering it subject to modification by arbitration only. He provided for the drafting of a Code of International Law and its amendment by unanimous vote of the Diet or Congress of Representatives.

Perhaps the most serious defect in his plan was the principle that sovereigns should be guaranteed against rebellions among their subjects—a cornerstone of the Holy Alliance in 1815.

The Plan of Jeremy Bentham

Jeremy Bentham, in *Fragment of an Essay on International Law* (1786–89), devised a plan to avert future wars comprising four fundamentals: reduction of armaments; "Permanent Court of Judicature" with powers of arbitration backed by sanctions of force; codification of international law; emancipation of all colonies.

The Plan of Immanuel Kant

Kant's *Zum Ewigen Frieden* (*Perpetual Peace*) (1795) contained an examination of reforms to be undertaken while war still existed, in order to create a public opinion favorable to the abolition of war, and suggestions for final organization of perpetual peace.

He contended that man was by nature selfish and base, but that mankind had risen to a high state of civilization through competition and mutual antagonisms of individuals in society, which had not only produced social chaos, but had also brought out all man's latent powers until the chaos had been resolved by the formation of the state. He foreshadowed an analogous development among states themselves, culminating in a "federation of free republics," meaning by "republic" any form of government embodying the liberty and equality of its subjects. Federation would involve surrender of a portion of power in return for participation in a wider, richer, more abundant life.

His practical measures concentrated on non-intervention in wars of other nations and the gradual abolition of standing armies. He made no detailed provisions for an international tribunal.

Kant's enduring contribution to the problem was that he lifted the discussion of war and peace above the level of politics and exalted it into a question of ethics and social conscience.

In the period before the American and French revolutions, there were other plans and proposals for maintaining peace. But these references will at least indicate the antiquity of peace yearnings.

This survey of these early methods of preserving peace shows that they are, dominantly, to keep it by military force. Such were the Pax Romana, the Great Design of Henry of Navarre, and some parts of the less belligerent plans. But in this early period there arose also some proposals for preserving peace by moral force, reason, good will, and international co-operation. Such were early agreements between cities, and much of the proposals of Gerohus, of Pierre Dubois, Dante, Emeric Crucé, William Penn, Saint-Pierre, J. J. Rousseau, Jeremy Bentham, and Immanuel Kant.

CHAPTER III

Movement of the Seven Dynamic Forces in the 140 Years before 1914

WE ARE NOT HERE concerned with military campaigns or battles. Therefore, we do not delay our readers with an account of the forty years of world-wide wars beginning with the American Revolution and ending with the defeat of Napoleon and the treaty of peace at the Congress of Vienna in 1815. Our concern is to follow as far as may be essential the movement of the seven dynamic forces over the 140 years up to the explosion of 1914. For, as we have said, it is from analysis of these forces and the manner in which statesmen dealt with them that we can gain both negative and positive experience in making and in preserving peace. We shall first briefly describe the movement of the pressures of ideologies; economic pressures; nationalism; imperialism; militarism; fear and its satellites, hate and revenge; together with the will to peace during this period; and then will sum up their relation to the world explosion in 1914.

The Ideological Forces[1]

Early in this period of 140 years ending in 1914 emerged the world-wide conflict of two fundamental and irreconcilable ideologies. On the one hand was the ideology of personal liberty[2] and representative government —and on the other, advocacy of various degrees of subjection or enslavement of the individual, whether by actual slavery, serfdom, or oppression by class, monarch, or state. Neither ideology is capable of precise definition, but it is necessary to introduce some definition in order to follow the conflict and its relation to war and peace.

The definition of personal liberty varies from time to time and from race to race, for it is modified by the whole racial history of peoples. But there are two essential common denominators.

The first common denominator is the concept of the dignity of man and his personal rights. And, included in this concept, is that these rights are an endowment by the Creator and are unalienable by the state or any other domination. This concept came from two urges. One was from the demand of men for intellectual and spiritual freedom—free speech and free worship; the second, equally potent, was the demand of men for an economic freedom in which they might choose their own callings, bargain for their own labor, and reap and hold the rewards from their own enterprise and efforts.

[1]For outline of these forces, see p. 12.

[2]We have generally adopted the expressions "personal liberty," "representative government," and "free nations," rather than the terms "Liberalism" and "democracy." These latter terms have come to be used for many purposes far from their original meanings and have often been adopted by advocates of other systems.

The second common denominator is the political foundation of government upon laws made by the people's freely chosen representatives and not by any arbitrary power.

This ideology of personal liberty based its faith of progress in spiritual, intellectual, and economic life upon the sum of individual accomplishment, not of governmental action.

The formulation of the American representative government was greatly influenced by the insistence of Locke, Montesquieu, and Rousseau that sovereign power must rest in the people, that they could delegate these powers to their representatives in legislative bodies, that legislative bodies could in turn entrust administration to executive officers, but that these executive officers are trustees who must not dictate policies or improperly influence the people's representatives, or that again would be autocratic government, dissolving the Social Contract.

While the functioning of representative government requires rule by the majority, yet it is not tyranny by the majority, as is so often stated. The primary foundation of representative government lies in the inalienable rights of the individual. And protest at the invasions of those rights swiftly turns the minority into a majority.

These protective ideas were even further reinforced by the Founding Fathers in America through the genius of their separation of judicial, legislative and executive powers and their Bill of Rights.

The ideology of subjection of the individual is even more difficult to define, for it has had a score of shapes and has changed them with the times. Its mildest common denominator is the idea that the purposes of the state take precedence over all personal liberties. Its more oppressive forms embrace all degrees of slavery, serfdom, or peonage. And this subjection of individual freedom is expressed in political organization not only based upon the Divine Right of Kings or dictators, but also by class government, whether military, aristocratic, landowning, ecclesiastic, or labor, or by a single political party.

No one can doubt the challenge of liberty to all peoples during the 140 years prior to the first World War. The success of the United States stimulated and inspired the entire world with the principles of representative government and inalienable rights. The forms of representative government spread over the whole Western Hemisphere. Britain, France, the Scandinavian states, the Low Countries, Switzerland, and Italy successfully developed it. Germany and Austria had made concessions to it. The ferment was active even in Russia, and the Czar had been compelled to yield to a Duma sporadic checks on arbitrary power. Japan and China were moving into this current. It rumbled in India, in Egypt and Turkey, and among the tribal Negroes of South Africa. Class government and aristocratic privilege were weakening everywhere.

Some degree of economic freedom long preceded the spread of spiritual and intellectual freedom and, indeed, was one of the greatest impulses to them. With increased production and wealth came the rise of the middle class, and this class was ceaselessly pushing for more intellectual and spiritual freedom and more political liberty.

The penetration of the concept of personal liberty over that period can also be measured in other terms. Slavery first fell into disrepute and then practically disappeared on the earth. Serfdom and peonage lived on only in a few still backward areas. Religious and intellectual freedom made wide progress even in the more reactionary nations.

Nevertheless, the old concepts held in central and eastern Europe and in Asia but were modified by time, and, finally, in the period we are discussing, prior to the first World War, for the most part simmered down to the subjection of the individual to class. Class government expressed itself in various forms: aristocratic, militaristic, or landowning.

Even in some liberal states, the catechism still carries the admonition to be content in the station in life to which it has pleased God to call us.

Individual liberty itself was modified by the Industrial Revolution from extreme *laissez faire* to a degree of intervention of the state to prevent economic abuse. That we shall discuss later. It can be said generally that in the clash between these two ideologies there was constant swing in the center of gravity between the authority of the state and the "inalienable" rights of the individual.

The important thing in great ideological changes is the direction in which they are moving. Certainly, personal liberty and representative government were moving forward over the whole world in this period prior to 1914.

We discuss the contribution of the systems of personal liberty and representative government to lasting peace later on. But here it may be said that this philosophic basis of life can flourish only in peace. The price of war to democracy is immediate surrender of personal freedom, with grave uncertainties as to its recovery after war. One purpose of this form of life is economic prosperity, and the consequence of war is its antithesis, impoverishment. Its foundation is the family, and the consequence of war is the sacrifice of its sons and brothers. From instinctive caution against these sacrifices there is inherent in representative government the live opposition to war.

And in representative government there is opportunity for opposition and thus far placing a brake upon war-makers.

The alarm of the other concepts and this rising tide of liberalism had no little part in the forces which led to the explosion of 1914.

Economic Forces[3]

The most important economic pressure bearing on peace and war during this period was the Industrial Revolution. Early in the century, the mercantile system had begun to yield to wider freedom of enterprise—from the combined pressures of the ideals of freedom, the invention of the steam engine, and from the philosophies of Adam Smith and his contemporaries.

Yet the revolutions which won the freedom of men had formulated their governmental framework to protect personal and political liberty. These governments were instituted in a climate of comparatively simple economic life. But from the very freedoms of mind and economic life which they provided came a second revolution. Out of free minds sprang a great flowering of scientific research and widening of knowledge of fundamental laws of nature. With the impulses of economic freedom, these discoveries and inventions were turned into huge tools of production, transportation, and communication. And with them came gigantic aggregations of capital and finance—the rise of modern capitalism. From these developments of technology and of mechanical power came a vast increase in the productivity of man, an unparalleled rise in the standard of living and comfort among all civilized races. And in turn, from these resources came an expansion of the hu-

[3]For outline of these forces, see p. 13.

manities. Art and music were made accessible to all; literature flourished; science developed rapidly; education was widespread; public health was studied and improved; and there were a thousand lesser manifestations of this trend. This progress and the constantly wider spread of intellectual, spiritual, and political freedom filled the hearts of men with hope and confidence. Men moved almost everywhere over the earth without fear or passports. Indeed, the last quarter of a century before the first World War may have been the golden age of good living. Certainly, despite the turn toward materialism, it was an age of confidence and hope.

In the light of experience of the past thirty years, however, we can see more clearly certain forces and clashes rising in the economic system that were to contribute to the great explosion of 1914. They were in the making before and in the golden age itself.

With the Industrial Revolution, civilization did turn dominantly to the materialistic side. The predominantly religious and spiritual character of the previous period greatly weakened.

The economic machine became infinitely more complicated and delicately balanced. International transportation and communications, finance, and trade brought enormous interchange and dependency among nations. A disruption anywhere in the world brought repercussions in stagnated markets and shocks in the flow of credit and capital, and finally, widespread unemployment.

Out of the economic system so intensified by the Machine Age grew a sort of rhythm of production and consumption, partly affected by credit movements and speculation, all of which brought periodic booms and slumps. In the boom, greed, speculation, and waste were rampant; and in the slump, the worker took the brunt in unemployment and misery, the farmer in inability to sell his products so vitally needed by the worker.

As we have said, the Industrial Revolution was superimposed upon the earlier revolution of political and personal liberty and its simpler economic frame. The two revolutions developed into sharp clashes over personal liberty. Out of the Machine Age grew forms of organization outside government which at times dominated the freedom of men. Pressure groups of labor, farmers, and business sprang up which interfered with government for their own selfish interest. The units of big business and big production and the groupings of finance around them penetrated into and dominated government. They were unfair in their treatment of and sharing with labor. Huge concentrations of finance and credit which were necessary to finance the advantageously huge industrial units brought their own train of evils. The control of finance and credit came to dominate free industry instead of merely serving as its lubricant. And the making of profit from sheer financial manipulation instead of production of commodities rose to a point of shrieking evil equally in the financial markets of London, Berlin, Paris, Petrograd, New York, Chicago, and a hundred lesser centers. Trade-union organization, a very necessary resistance by the workers to the domination of their lives and livelihoods by huge industrial units, in itself established dominations over freedom of men and made for inflexibilities and waste in the economic system.

Before the World War of 1914, the American people were slowly awakening to the necessity to correct these abuses and to become masters in their own house. That sort of *laissez faire* which struck at the freedom of men was not part of true liberty. However, abuses were being slowly corrected through regulation by specific law. Credit was being organized to modify the swing of the economic cycle. The growth of ethical concepts within most economic groupings was maturing. But before these problems could be solved, the first World War threw terrific shocks into these delicate balances of world economy and the movements of reform.

These weaknesses and clashes in the economic system had less consequence in producing the first World War than in the degeneration which followed it. But other economic pressures had very direct effect in bringing on the war of 1914. They came from the pressures of intensified populations in manufacturing countries for elbow room and markets. This contributed in turn to vast increases of armament and military rivalry. Especially in Britain, Germany, Italy, and Japan, industrialization made the people dependent upon imports for food and raw materials. The consequence was an enormous growth and rivalry in navies with which to safeguard the flow of supplies. This dependence upon imports and exports and the desire for elbow room greatly stimulated imperialism in the direction of control of colonial areas so as to secure independent sources of supplies and outlets for population. It stimulated economic and intellectual penetration into countries politically independent while possessed of sources of supplies and materials, in an effort to keep them friendly and co-operative. Thus, it intensified the drive of power politics into every corner of the world.

The Beginnings of Ideologies Hostile to Personal Liberty and Representative Government. Into this scene, while representative government was freeing the world from the overhang of medieval reactionary ideas of absolutism, militarist dictatorship, and domination of the state or class, a new shape of hostile ideology was to come into being. Karl Marx's *Das Kapital* had its immediate practical impulse from the Industrial Revolution and its theoretical basis in Hegel's philosophic glorification of the state. The ideology was not new in history, indeed it was very old, but it was largely formalized by Marx and his followers. And in furtherance of it, we witnessed the birth of a blood brother, Communism. The major distinction between the Socialists and the Communists was that Socialism was to be applied by parliamentary action, whereas Communism was to be applied by revolution and "dictatorship of the proletariat."

They both gave a beautiful blueprint of Utopia to the masses suffering from the hard masters of European industrialism and the pull and haul of the economic system. And inherent in these ideas was again the subjection of the individual to the state—again the apparition of the Middle Ages. These systems were basically more materialistic than the systems of liberty, because their whole thesis was to make a god of economic equality and to lessen intellectual and spiritual liberty. Socialism and Communism were to guarantee security without risk and all human blessings without that striving which the Lord laid upon Adam.

In the rapid growth of wealth and comfort, the condition of the worker did not sink as Marx prophesied. It rose. However, these ideas secured a hold on limited groups of theoretical intellectuals throughout the world, and the influence of their preachings did confuse liberal thought and add to the difficulties of representative government striving to solve the clashes within its own house. They, in some places, infected liberty by introducing government into the operation of and dictation to economic life, instead of regulating abuses by law. And thus freedom began the surrender to the state.

After the first World War, these ideologies were to take a high place in disruption of the world and to play a huge part in deepening this crisis in civilization.

NATIONALISM[4]

The 140 years prior to 1914 mark the period of greatest growth of nationalistic spirit in all history. The Renaissance, the Reformation, the growth of liberty and economic progress all contributed to a revival in racial interests and a yearning for self-government. And that desire was well stimulated by the hard heel of oppression.

In the Western Hemisphere during this 140 years, independence came to the United States, Argentina, Brazil, Uruguay, Paraguay, Bolivia, Peru, Chile, Ecuador, Colombia, Venezuela, Costa Rica, Panama, Nicaragua, Honduras, Guatemala, Haiti, Santo Domingo, El Salvador, Cuba, and Mexico. In the Eastern Hemisphere, Belgium, Greece, Rumania, Bulgaria, Serbia, and Montenegro gained their independence. Other races rebelled and failed. Such was the fate of Poland, Finland, and Hungary. Later, it is true, Hungary was joined to Austria by a personal union and, in some respects, was the dominant partner in the Dual Empire. Altogether, some twenty-seven new nations emerged in this period, prior to 1914. Germany and Italy achieved national unity. Almost all of these changes were the result of wars, and

[4]For outline of this force, see p. 13.

the very privations of the struggle solidified the nationalist spirit of the liberated countries.

Of the more capable submerged races, the Irish, the Finns, the Estonians, the Latvians, the Lithuanians, the Poles, the Czechs, the Slovaks, the Slovenes, the Croats, the Dalmatians, the Georgians, the Azerbaijanese, the Armenians, the Arabs, the Egyptians and the peoples of India and Malaysia were still subject to foreign rule. And in some cases, their oppression not only took the form of exploitation, but also bitter restriction of racial cultures. In the desire of the conquerors of many of them to break down rising nationalism among them, their native language, literature, education, and all national manifestations were suppressed with a heavy hand. These very oppressions hardened them not only for physical rebellion, but for intellectual resistance.

And the racial yearnings for independence produced action upon still another stage. Over Europe there were many areas where the races were mixed—the "irredentas." Fragments of the French, the Poles, and the Danes were under Germany; Greeks under Turkey and Bulgaria; Serbians and Rumanians under Austria-Hungary; and so on. Any boundaries athwart the areas of mixed population leave great masses of people separated from their homelands. The dominating governments on both sides of such boundaries invariably endeavor to minimize or extinguish these alien cultures and institutions and to absorb them into the dominant race. Their homelands are stirred in sympathy and hate.

These were all areas of ferment for freedom. And these racial frictions extended even further. There were racial groupings, such as the Slavs, for whom Russia professed a guardianship as far afield as the Adriatic.

Germany professed to take foreign groups of Germanic origins under her protection.

Within the pressures of these nationalistic forces and their strivings were huge stores of powder ready for the great explosion of 1914.

IMPERIALISM[5]

The movement of imperialism in the 140 years prior to the World War of 1914 and the clashes it produced were to bring portentous consequences in war and peace. Within it were the old urges to power, glory, and exploitation of other races. But the Industrial Revolution added still further urges. Modern education, periodicals, movies, quicker modes of travel and communication, closer contact with neighbors all stimulated knowledge of higher standards of living elsewhere. The Industrial Revolution immensely stimulated the growth of populations, created an urge for more elbow room. As we have said, it brought great pressures for outlets of surplus goods and an assurance of overseas supplies of raw materials. Surplus capital sought areas to develop.

All these hopes and purposes were advanced by expansion in conquest of colonies or the occupation of backward races and vacant spaces.

The imperial movement in these 140 years was the greatest of all history. Beyond the coastal settlements in North America, Australasia, and Africa there were either open spaces or lands held by backward races waiting to be occupied and divided. India, the East Indies, and parts of China were open to be taken by conquest.

Under the varied pressures of rivalry, weakness, and

[5]For outline of this force, see p. 17.

expansive energy, vast empires were to rise and fall. The part this development of empire played in war and peace and its continuing pressure can be indicated from a short review of these imperial growths and decays.

Within this period, the Spanish Empire almost disappeared. At the beginning, it embraced all of South America with the exception of Brazil; all Central America, Mexico, Texas, and a great sweep of territory westward to include California; and Florida to the east. It included Cuba, Puerto Rico, Guam, and the Philippines—a vast empire of well over six million square miles. At the end of this period, Spain held but a scrap of a great empire. Her incapacity in colonial government, her hard exploitation of the people, and rising demand for liberty cost her all her holdings in North, Central, and South America by revolutions for independence. The United States took Florida from her by annexation in 1819; Cuba, Puerto Rico, Guam and the Philippines by war in 1898. There remained to her only the minor appendages of Spanish Morocco, Rio de Oro and Fernando Po, Cape Juby, and Spanish Guinea. Territorially, the greatest empire in history had gone out of business.

The Portuguese Empire, which had once shared the world with Spain under a ruling from the Pope, began this period with vast possessions, including the Azores, Portuguese East and West Africa, Brazil, and various holdings in the Far East. During these years it saw the shrinkage of these holdings, and in 1822 Brazil set up its independent existence. At the end of the period, however, Portugal still remained an empire of 838,000 square miles, with 14,500,000 people, including the important territories of Angola and Mozambique and various small outposts in India, China, and Malaya.

The Dutch had long rivaled the English as a sea power. But in this period they lost Penang, Singapore, Malacca, Ceylon, Cape Colony, and part of Borneo to the British. They, however, even as the weaker sea power, managed to keep a very considerable empire, including the Netherlands Indies, composed of Java, Sumatra, Celebes, part of Borneo, and a host of islands, as well as Dutch Guiana and Curaçao in the Western Hemisphere. Altogether, the Dutch Empire in 1914 comprised some 800,000 square miles, with 41,000,000 people.

Belgium was a late-comer in the imperial class when, in 1885, she set up the Congo Free State, an important territory of over 900,000 square miles, giving her a total population of 17,000,000 people.

Italy, during the early part of this period, was engaged in the process of national unification of the Italian states. She ventured into overseas imperialism by an attempted expansion in Abyssinia, which failed (1885–89), and the conquest of Eritrea, Tripoli, and Italian Somaliland, which succeeded.

During this period, Russia was in steady growth. She gained what were later called Estonia, Latvia, Lithuania, Finland, and a large part of Poland, the Crimea, the Caucasus, and Bessarabia by conquest. She expanded across Siberia to the Pacific. In the relatively short period from 1850 to 1914, Russia, despite some losses to Japan, had acquired an area of 3,250,000 square miles, and in 1914 governed 170,000,000 people.

Turkey began the period as a large, if unwieldy and loosely knit empire holding Rumania, Bulgaria, Serbia, Montenegro, Albania, Macedonia, Arabia, Egypt, Armenia, Greece, Crete, Smyrna, Cyprus, Syria, Palestine, Mesopotamia, Algeria, and Tunisia. She lost Algeria and Tunisia to the French; Tripoli to the Italians; and Egypt to the British. Revolutions for independence cost her Rumania, Serbia, Montenegro, Bulgaria, and Greece. In spite of all these losses, Turkey arrived at the first World War as a considerable imperial power, holding Syria, Smyrna and Arabia, Palestine, and part of Armenia.

Japan was one of the last Powers to begin an imperial career. She seized Korea. She won Dairen and half of Sakhalin from the Russians and parts of Manchuria, Shantung, Formosa, and the Pescadores from China. In 1914 her imperialism was burning brightly.

The French Empire underwent many changes. Shortly before this period began, France lost to Great Britain almost the whole of her great colonial empire in North America as well as in the West Indies and India. During this period, she sold the Louisiana Territory to the United States. These losses were partly compensated by the successive acquisition of Algeria, French Equatorial Africa, Cochin China, Cambodia, Annam, Dahomey, Tunis, Tonkin, Madagascar, and many lesser possessions. She ended the period with 4,000,000 square miles of colonial territory.

The Austro-Hungarian Empire emerged from the Napoleonic Wars with Austria, Hungary, Bohemia, Slovakia, Galicia, Croatia, Slovenia, Transylvania, Dalmatia, and broad stretches of Italian territory. It lost the Italian provinces in the unification of Italy but managed to hold the rest and later annexed Bosnia and Herzegovina. Austria did not endeavor to become an overseas empire.

Germany confined her imperialistic energies to the continent of Europe in the earlier part of the period.

She united all the chief German areas except Austria and the Sudetenland. She obtained part of Poland, Alsace-Lorraine, and a bit of Denmark by various wars. In 1884, she annexed German East Africa and German Southwest Africa; also Togoland, the Cameroons, and German New Guinea. Kiaochow was taken by Germany from the Chinese in 1898. In 1914, German imperialism was clearly on the march.

Great Britain shows the greatest of all imperial expansions in this period of 140 years prior to the World War of 1914. Before that time she possessed, aside from the rebellious American colonies, the greater part of Canada and most of her West Indies possessions. She held a minor part of India. By successive conquests she acquired Ceylon, Hong Kong, Natal, Cape Colony, part of Borneo, the Straits Settlements, the Falkland islands, the Transvaal, Orange Free State, Trinidad, Egypt, the Sudan, Ashanti, Burma, and the Shan States. She occupied Australasia, British West Africa, Nigeria, Somaliland, Rhodesia, Uganda, Nyasaland. She expanded over western Canada, almost the whole of India, and the Malay States. She acquired numbers of islands and military bases. At the end of the period she occupied about 12,000,000 square miles with a population of 475,000,000. And she had demonstrated the greatest capacity for colonial administration in history.

Our own American territorial growth should not be overlooked. By the Louisiana Purchase we acquired the vast Midwest and part of the Mountain States, extending from Canada to the Gulf of Mexico. We seized Florida, Puerto Rico, Guam, and the Philippine Islands from Spain, and New Mexico, Arizona, Nevada, and California from Mexico. Texas was admitted to the

Union. We expanded over Oregon and Washington and some Pacific islands. We purchased Alaska, and Hawaii joined us voluntarily.

American expansion overseas, as events have shown, can hardly be called imperialism. We took Cuba and gave it independence. Far from exploiting the Philippines, we poured money into them for more than forty years. We brought up successive generations on the Declaration of Independence, "Give me liberty or give me death," and the rights of the individual. The inevitable result was the demand for independence, to which we agreed. And now we have seen Filipino troops fighting side by side with our own.

Thus we see that in this period Spain decayed as an imperial Power; Portugal and Turkey lost ground; the Netherlands, Russia, France, Germany, Japan, Britain, and the United States expanded in varying degrees.

There is no doubt that imperialism was a gigantic force in world affairs during this period. Its frictions and pressures nowhere made for peace. And these pressures of imperialism had much to do with the explosion of 1914.

MILITARISM[6]

As stated in defining the force of militarism, we are here considering only the spirit of military organization as a force in itself. The necessity of organization for defense in a world swarming with aggressive races needs no justification. But it must not be overlooked that even such defense organization often develops a military caste whose sole life outlet is war. In order to reduce this danger, the representative governments have always in-

[6]For outline of this force, see p. 15.

sisted upon the subjection of the military to the civilian arm of the government and its exclusion from policy making. But not so under non-representative forms of government.

In the period under discussion, two profound examples of militarism developed, the one in France, the other in Germany. There can be no doubt of the sheer militarism in Napoleon. His very phrases burst with war and the glory of war. Militarism developed in the German race partly as the repercussion of repeated French invasions and was successfully organized under Frederick the Great. He was the warlord as well as the head of the state. And his successors perpetuated this idea. There also arose a group of German philosophers who extolled military service as a foundation of moral development and iron discipline as a part of "culture." They eulogized military action as the highest expression of race.

None of this was new in history. Sparta had brought ruin upon liberal Greece by just such philosophy and organization.

Europe became a network of military alliances glaring at one another. The Triple Alliance of Germany, Austria, and Italy was constantly rattling its swords. Counter to them grew up an alliance between Russia and France with British support. And the Balkans allied and counter-allied themselves under inspirations from the greater alliances. During the century after the demobilization following the Congress of Vienna in 1814, the armies and navies of the world increased far more rapidly than the growth of population.

The greatest growth of military establishments took place in Germany, Russia, Austria, and France. Japan was at this time somewhat less aggressive, although here the military held authority equal to the civil authority, on which they gradually encroached.

The chips on all these shoulder-straps and the stupid, arrogant, and aggressive minds that flaunted them gave warning that powder trains were being laid for the gigantic explosion of 1914.

Hate, Fear, and Revenge[7]

Hate and its kinsmen, fear and revenge, were not inactive forces in international life during these 140 years. Our own feeling of hostility for the British, born with the Revolution, stimulated by the war of 1812, did not fade until after the Spanish-American War. After that it lingered on in suspicion and constantly kept alive our naval building.

A combined hate-fear-and-revenge complex against Germany dominated all French policies after the humiliation of the Franco-Prussian War of 1870 and the seizure of Alsace-Lorraine. These emotions bred the alliance with Russia and the entente with Britain. Frequent wars between France and Britain over 300 years had built a hate that only faded because of the common menace of Germany.

Russia generated a profound dislike of Austria for her designs upon the Slav races, for which Russia considered herself the protector.

Italian hate and fear of France, because of her intrigues to prevent unification of Italy and the thwarting of Italian African colonial ambitions, kept Italy's suspicions aflame and eventually threw her into military alliance with Germany and Austria.

[7]For outline of these forces, see p. 19.

The Germans generated a hate for Britain and British supremacy in empire and trade which gave birth to the expression "der Tag." Germany and Austria entered into military alliance largely out of fear of Russia.

The very rise and decay of the great empires produced constant hates and suspicions.

There were lesser hates: Hungary against Rumania; Greece against Serbia; Greece, Bulgaria, and Rumania against Turkey; the Poles against Germans, Russians, and Austrians. Generally, there were hates toward their oppressors in all the submerged states and racial minorities. And we were to see in this period the growth of another great fear—the fear of interruption of overseas food supplies and raw materials and markets among the industrial nations—and this fear found rest only in expanding the rival navies.

All these emotions profoundly affected international relations and were ready to explode with any lighted match.

CHAPTER IV

Movement of the Seven Dynamic Forces in the 140 Years before 1914

(*Continued*)

The Will to Peace[1]

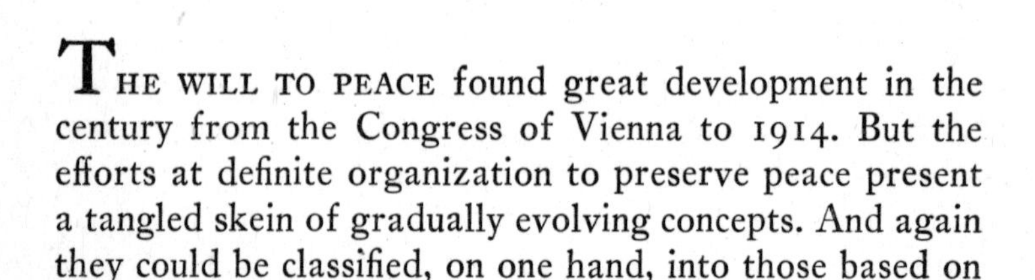

THE WILL TO PEACE found great development in the century from the Congress of Vienna to 1914. But the efforts at definite organization to preserve peace present a tangled skein of gradually evolving concepts. And again they could be classified, on one hand, into those based on military force, and those relying upon pacific means of law, morals, and reason.

Among the developments of a more positive order during this period, aside from the balance of power, were the Holy Alliance and the Quadruple Alliance of 1815, the Monroe Doctrine of 1823, the Hague Conferences, the broader concept of the Concert of Europe, and various military alliances. With the spread of personal liberty and representative government, there followed a fruitful period in the development of international law, of international co-operation, and the creation of methods of settling controversy by peaceful means.

[1]For outline of this force, see p. 20.

The Holy Alliance

The Congress of Vienna met in 1814 to put an end to the forty years of world wars bred by the ideas emerging from the American and French revolutions. Its general principle was the restoration, so far as possible, of the situation prior to those wars. The general philosophy was the *status quo ante* and Talleyrand's Legitimist Restoration—that is, the Divine Right of legitimate emperors and kings. The concepts of liberty, with their principles of the right of self-determination of nations and of rights of nationalism to all peoples, were hotly repudiated. Metternich believed peace could best be maintained by "the vigilant benevolence of the allied sovereigns."

History stated in the usual terms of military victory and defeat is often entirely misleading. The Congress of Vienna marked a decisive Allied victory over revolutionary France, and this victory was intended to set the clock back and restore conditions as they were before the world was troubled by disturbing thoughts of human freedom. The victory was clear and the treaty was clear, but there is no escaping the fact that the very ideas of liberty, which had supposedly been defeated, largely dominated Europe during the next century in complete disregard of what had been signed and sealed.

Out of this conference came the Holy Alliance, which was a short-lived attempt to maintain peace and order upon certain high principles. The great sovereigns agreed to "remain united by the bonds of a true and indissoluble fraternity, . . . they will, on all occasions and in all places, lend each other aid and assistance . . . to protect Religion, Peace, and Justice."

They further "solemnly declared . . . in their political relations with every other government, to take for their sole guide the precepts of that holy religion, namely, the Precepts of Justice, Christian Charity, and Peace. . . ."

The pact concluded with an invitation to all Powers who might "choose solemnly to avow the sacred principles which have dictated this act" to become members of "this Holy Alliance." It was a sort of 1815 version of the Kellogg-Briand Pact of a strictly personal character between three absolute sovereigns.

The signatories can hardly be accused of having followed these principles. Alexander of Russia alone seems to have taken it at all seriously. There is no reason to doubt the sincerity of this mystic. The Emperor of Austria signed in a scoffing mood after remarking that "if it was a question of politics, he must refer it to his chancellor, if of religion, to his confessor." Metternich's approval was limited to calling it a "loud-sounding nothing." Castlereagh was kinder in referring to it as "a piece of sublime mysticism and nonsense." Although the King was restored in France, from the start the French Government treated the Holy Alliance with contempt.

The Alliance was in fact a sort of personal league of sovereigns with no definite plan or procedure, and its real purpose was to justify foreign intervention in the affairs of any state threatened with revolution.

The actual achievements of the Holy Alliance were not great. The Emperor of Russia did intervene to help the Greek rebels against the Ottoman Empire, and as late as 1848 he sent an army to Hungary to suppress Kossuth. But the policy of intervention split with British opposition and upon the rock of the American Monroe Doctrine. As an effective force it lasted a very short time.

The Quadruple Alliance (1815)

Out of the Holy Alliance, however, the practical gentlemen a few months later produced the Quadruple Alliance.

This agreement is sometimes confused with the Holy Alliance. The latter was merely a statement of high aims and motives, whereas the Quadruple Alliance was a working arrangement for dealing with European problems. It was signed on November 20, 1815, by Austria, Great Britain, Prussia, and Russia. It was responsible for calling the four great European congresses which dealt with the troubled situation from the Congress of Vienna until 1822. These were the congresses at Aix-la-Chapelle (1818), Troppau (1820), Laibach (1821), and Verona (1822). The Quadruple Alliance had clear and obvious aims. It existed primarily to hold the *status quo* and bolster up the doctrine of legitimacy which had been seriously undermined by the upheavals of the revolutionary period. To this end it directed considerable energy to the suppression of growing Liberalism and nationalism.

These methods were carried to such an extreme that the British Government could not accept the protocol of Troppau providing that, "States which have undergone a change of government due to revolution, the results of which threaten other States, *ipso facto* cease to be members of the European Alliance, and remain excluded from it until their situation gives guarantees for legal order and stability. If, owing to such alterations, immediate danger threatens other States, the Powers bind themselves, by peaceful means, or if need be by arms, to bring back the guilty State into the bosom of the Great Alliance."

The Balance of Power

These plans growing out of the Congress of Vienna were, however, ultimately absorbed into the balance of power and the Concert of Europe.

The origins of the principle of the balance of power are lost in the mists of history. Grotius formulated the idea clearly as a fundamental principle. According to him, it was in the common interest and it was the right and duty of all nations to go to war if the balance of power was menaced.

The balance of power is not a principle of law, but rather a principle of action with the claim that it was a law of nature. Its essential base is to maintain a situation where nations modify their aggressiveness by fear of defeat. Fear of defeat always modifies aggressiveness—even in the jungle.

We must remember that the theory of the balance of power recognized the collective right of Europe to peace and freedom from territorial aggression. It recognized a collective interest in preventing undue expansion by any nation. It has often been said that the system had not often been called into operation to resist military invasions. This is perhaps true, but the fear of its operation gives it a long record of successful retarding of such aggression.

The practice of the balance of power fundamentally rested on groupings and periodic regroupings to hold three most important aggressive centers in restraint. They were France, the German-dominated Central Empires, and Russia. The minor states revolved mostly around these suns.

Britain played a major but outside part in these affairs. And she was the determining weight in the balance of power. Her empire and her life are curiously exposed in a military sense, and she must depend very largely upon sea power and upon diplomacy—power politics—for her protection. Her face has always been turned toward the seven seas and her colonial activities far from Europe. But she is only twenty miles away from the Continent, and her safety requires that the shores of the channel and the North Sea remain in friendly hands. Furthermore, her prosperity is closely interwoven with peace on the Continent. Thus, economic and political dangers have periodically thrust her back into continental action, little as she may have liked it.

Her major method has, for centuries, been to maintain a dominant navy, and when power groups develop which threaten aggression on the Continent, to throw her weight with the weaker side. This has become a sort of law of British nature.

These balances have periodically broken into war, and then, after each costly experience, Britain retreats into a fit of isolation—until driven out again by some new menacing combination.

All this has given to British policy a strong color of opportunism, not perhaps the opportunism of carelessness, but of carefully thought out policy. She knows what is good for her today, but realizes better than most countries the inevitability of shifting balances and change. And this accounts for a striking British characteristic, an invincible reluctance to bind herself as regards unforeseen eventualities.

Continental Powers are given to criticizing British policy for its apparent inconsistencies. But Britain usually shows complete consistency even in her apparent lack of logic or continued affiliations. The oft-expressed continental phrase is, "Perfidious Albion." But Americans can well sympathize with her fits of isolationism, her reluctance to get into continental wars, and yet her necessity to fend off danger by preventing any power from becoming too dominant.

A moment's glance at the history of Europe during the 140-year period shows a series of examples of these shifting balances and crises, although they have been at times obscured by national upheavals and the surge of personal freedom and representative government. There were the combinations of practically the whole of Europe against French aggression under Napoleon. There was a manifestation in the Crimean War of 1853–56, where England, France, and Austria supported Turkey against Russian aggression. After the Franco-Prussian War in 1870, the rising unification of Germany and her drive for colonies and the growth of her navy began to alarm Britain, and in reaction, Bismarck sought strength from an alliance with Russia and Austria. Within a few years Russia withdrew from this triple alliance, but in a very short time Italy, aroused by the French seizure of Tunis, took Russia's place. This German-Austrian-Italian alliance continued until 1914. Britain stayed out of these alliances until 1904, but in 1898, when there was a threat of war between Britain and France over the Sudan, Britain went so far as to explore the possibilities of an alliance with Germany.

The intensity of French fears, and hatred of Germany for the loss of Alsace-Lorraine in 1870, led her to build industriously a grouping for her own protection. In 1895, France and Russia had made an alliance directed toward the Triple Alliance group, and in 1904, the British loosely joined this group through the Triple Entente.

There is no doubt that alliances in general are not lasting, that they are constantly subject to attempts to dissolve them or to face them with superior force. They always build for competitive armament. All of this leads to unrest and insecurity. Although the balance of power is described as a "just equilibrium," governments are constantly seeking to secure not so much an even balance as preponderance for their own side, and this leads to ultimate conflict. And the effect of these combinations is to make war on a much wider front by drawing in many nations not directly part of the controversy. This was essentially the case in 1914.

But whatever the shortcomings of the system of balance of power, there is no doubt that the ability of the Powers to hold each other in check has gone far at times to avert aggression and violence.

It is a mistake to think of the balance of power as belonging to the past or even to Europe. It dominated Europe after Versailles despite its presumed burial by the League of Nations. And it is as alive today as it ever was.

The Concert of Europe

Out of all these dangers grew a new movement—the Concert of Europe. It marked a feeble growth of general collective action for maintenance of peace—that is, a Council of Nations. It was not an institution but a practice, a practice which automatically grew out of the Holy Alliance and the Quadruple Alliance with the body of decisions remaining from the four great congresses which followed from the latter. These congresses had in emergencies brought the great Powers into consultation to keep the peace as best they could. It was not an agreement, but rather a loose system which simply prevailed.

At the close of the Crimean War—in the 1850s—the Concert of European Powers concluded a number of further agreements with a view to establishing orderly processes of international life. Although the organization of the Concert had never been embodied in treaty agreements, it was clearly recognized, and Turkey was in 1853 specifically admitted to the advantages of "public law and the Concert of Europe."

The same Powers in 1864 signed the Geneva Convention, creating the Red Cross System. In 1874, the laws and customs of war on land were embodied in the Brussels Convention. In 1878, the Concert of Powers at the Congress of Berlin drew up a treaty reconciling the claims of Turkey, Greece, and the Balkan States—at least tiding over the emergency.

The Concert was most active in the period after the Franco-Prussian War, no doubt finding its chief worry in the growing militarism of the German Empire. All the elements of war were present from 1870 to 1914, but war was averted. The Powers remained in constant contact on the thousand and one everyday causes of friction. When a crisis came, the Concert foregathered directly or by communications and arrived at some sort of settlement, as, for instance, in dealing with China during the Boxer crisis of 1900, and with Morocco in 1906 at the Algeciras Conference. The United States took part in both these settlements.

The Concert may not have been greatly concerned with the rights of small countries, but controversies were settled and crises were tided over by this sort of Council of Nations.

It was a precarious way of keeping the peace, and there was always danger that the system would fail. And when it did finally fail in 1914, the failure was due to the accumulation of explosive forces beyond the powers of this form of diplomacy. Or at least statesmanship was so weak as to fail to recognize them.

The Monroe Doctrine

Surprisingly enough, the Monroe Doctrine may be listed with the tried methods of keeping the peace and, more surprisingly, it must be listed among the methods for keeping the peace by force. But it was in itself a participation in the balance of power, for the United States thereby threw its weight to any Western Hemisphere state threatened with European encroachment.

There is no doubt that it depended on force, for it was heeded only because it was known that the armed strength of the United States was behind the President's warning, to make it effective.

When we speak of this force, we must also remember that America did not stand alone behind the Doctrine. There was the interest of Britain in maintaining it as part of the balance of power among European empires, not because Britain supported or even referred to the Monroe Doctrine, but because there happened to be a coincidence of interest which led Canning to declare that Britain could not see with indifference the change in balance by the transfer of any of Spain's possessions to another Power.

The essential part of President Monroe's warning to the Powers of Europe was his statement that "we should consider any attempt on their part to extend their system to any portion of this Hemisphere as dangerous to our peace and safety." Aside from its political implications in defense of the United States, the Doctrine was prompted by the ideological cleavage between the two hemispheres. The interest of the Holy Alliance in support of Spain and its insistence on Divine Right were as repugnant to us as American agitation for personal liberty and representative government must have been horrifying to the statesmen of Europe bent on putting down such shocking ideas.

Two notable incidents arose in connection with this Doctrine. The first was the landing of British, French, and Spanish troops in Mexico in 1861 and the proclamation of Maximilian as Emperor. Engaged in civil war, we were too weak to act at once, but in 1866 we put an end to it. A further action was taken in 1895 in protection of Venezuela from British threats and demands.

At times we went far afield in our interpretations of the Doctrine, especially in the administration of President Theodore Roosevelt. That stretch of interpretation covered the idea that we must keep these Western Hemisphere nations in order to prevent pretexts for European intervention. And with this color of authority, we justified numbers of military and diplomatic interventions on our part to establish internal order and to enforce the commercial contracts of our neighbors. These actions created great fears and resentment against the United States. During the Coolidge Administration, Secretary of State Hughes came out vigorously against this entire conception of the Doctrine, got the Marines out of Santo Domingo, and took the first steps toward getting them out of Nicaragua. To bring this situation definitely to an end, Mr. Hoover, then President-elect, visited the South

American governments in 1928 and gave public assurances to them of an entire change in these policies. To emphasize it, he at once directed the withdrawal of American troops from Nicaragua and Haiti. He directed the publication of a memorandum by Under Secretary of State J. Reuben Clark repudiating the whole thesis of intervention which had been built up. This attitude has been maintained and developed by Mr. Roosevelt's Administration under the name of the "Good Neighbor" policy.

In the large sense, the Monroe Doctrine has worked beneficially to maintain separation of Western Hemisphere problems from those of Europe and has contributed to preserve peace in the world.

The Development of Law and International Co-operation

The last half of the nineteenth century marked the great advance in ideas of international law and international co-operation alongside the older forces of balance of power, the Concert of Europe, and the Monroe Doctrine. Indeed, the Concert of Europe played some part in this development, but it was primarily due to the spread of representative government. Inherent in that thesis are government by law and the popular demand for peace. The strength of the movement came from those countries where there was representative government and where the people had a voice. There were faint efforts to champion the same ideas in other countries—but the popular demand for orderly methods in the conduct of international relations was in direct proportion to the popular share in government. At first these attempts to formulate the demand for better-organized peace were only occasional and fragmentary—but as the years went by, the movement grew in volume. We may note some of the more important incidents which mark its progress.

Pan American Union

On May 24, 1888, the United States Congress, as a result of efforts begun by Secretary of State Blaine in 1881, passed an act authorizing the President to summon a conference of the independent nations of the Western Hemisphere. Thus was formulated the great ideal for which Bolivar strove. This conference was to be called for the purpose of considering measures to preserve the peace and promote the prosperity of the several American nations, to establish economic co-operation, and to include a definite plan for arbitration of all disputes between them. These Pan-American conferences met a common need and have long played an important role in the improvement of inter-American relations.

The several succeeding conferences gradually led to the founding of the Pan American Union in 1910. The Union performs valuable statistical and informational services, follows up the decisions of the conferences, and arranges their programs. A long list of treaties bearing upon economic, cultural, and peace promotion has been perfected.

But above all, the Pan American Union has served a useful purpose, in the preservation of peace, through the governing board meeting round a table once a month. It has been able to smooth over many difficulties as they have arisen and thus avoid more serious disputes.

The Hague Conferences

The first fundamental and courageous attack upon the world problems of peace and war was made by the first Hague Peace Conference, called in 1899 by the Emperor of Russia. While it is customary to belittle the work of the first Hague Conference for not going far enough, it must be admitted, in the light of subsequent experience, that its achievements were remarkable in laying a foundation for further progress.

The conference, attended by the representatives of twenty-six countries, resulted in the signature of three important Conventions:

1. A Convention for the Pacific Settlement of International Disputes which set up as an agency a Permanent Court of Arbitration at the Hague, with a permanent organization and a defined procedure for arbitration and inquiry.
2. A Convention Respecting the Laws and Customs of War on Land. This Convention confirmed previous agreements and marked a notable progress in building up a body of international law. The fact that this Convention has been repeatedly and cynically violated does not destroy its value. Its wise provisions still stand and will serve to guide us when we recover our balance.
3. A Convention for the Adaptation to Maritime Warfare of the Principles of the Geneva Convention of August 22, 1864.

In further development of the principle of arbitration of international controversies, a plan was proposed for obligatory arbitration of all questions excepting those "involving vital interests and national honor." It was found impossible to conclude a convention against the strong opposition of Germany, who claimed that these reservations reduced it to nothing.

The second Hague Peace Conference, convened in 1907, was attended by the representatives of forty-four countries and further perfected the procedures in arbitration and the Conventions signed at the first conference. Thirteen Conventions were signed and in large part ratified by important Powers.

In the first thirty-eight years of its existence, there were twenty-one arbitrations before tribunals of the Permanent Court or before special tribunals of such character as to be listed in the reports of the Administrative Council of the Court.

London Conference of 1909

Convention XII of the second Hague Conference initiated discussion upon the constitution of an International Prize Court. In 1909, the British Government called a conference in London upon the law to be applied by such a Court composed of representatives of nine leading maritime nations. This conference drew up a document known as the "Declaration of London."

The Declaration confirmed the terms of the Declaration of Paris of 1856 that a blockade to be binding must be effective. It was the beginning of world demand for clear freedom of the seas during war. It laid down agreed definitions of contraband of war and unneutral service and prescribed rules governing the capture or destruction of neutral prizes and the transfer of ships to a neutral flag, with further rules concerning enemy character, convoy, and resistance to search. The British House of Lords failed to take action on this declaration, which has consequently never become a binding convention, but has nevertheless influenced the development of the law.

Development of Arbitration and Mediation

In 1911, during the Taft Administration, treaties were negotiated with Great Britain and France extending the principle of arbitration to all justiciable questions. These treaties were materially amended by the Senate, and President Taft declined to accept them in amended form, so they did not become effective. They serve chiefly to indicate the direction of progress.

Mr. Bryan, during his term of office as Secretary of State (1913–15), made a definite contribution to the cause of conciliation. He proposed the acceptance of a period of delay and independent investigation and report before resort to war, and concluded a series of treaties incorporating this idea. He prescribed that whenever the methods of diplomacy were found unable to adjust a dispute, it should be submitted for investigation and report to an International Commission, and that the contracting parties should agree not to declare war or begin hostilities during the period of such investigation and report. This in itself insured a cooling-off period which might readily be prolonged by the proceedings of the Commission of Inquiry. This was primarily useful for disputed questions of fact. A number of such treaties were negotiated.

International Unions

During this period can be noted the growth of international unions which have been conspicuously successful in building up international co-operation in fields where it was useful and in the common interest.

First and foremost of these, of course, is the Universal Postal Union, established in 1874 and now comprising every recognized state.

Other unions which follow the same methods for varying numbers of states are the Telegraphic Union; the Metric Union; the Union for the Protection of Submarine Cables; Radio and Communications Union; the Union for the Repression of the White Slave Trade; the Union for the Protection of Industrial Property.

The Transformation of Diplomacy

During this period of 140 years, diplomatic activity was itself transformed from its older dominant occupation with alliances, intrigues, and social contacts into the major purpose of preventing and allaying friction and controversy. Diplomacy is in everyday operation in every capital. It finds its strength in the give and take of ordinary life. By its very elasticity it settles 999 out of 1,000 conflicts or possible conflicts. It was to fill in where diplomacy fails that all the stronger methods were developed. In sequence, there have developed regular diplomatic steps in the use of the "good offices" of other nations; conciliation and mediation with examination and report on the facts by friendly nations; arbitration by independent agencies; or judicial decision of some types of controversy.

The differences between arbitration and judicial decision are perhaps more practical than theoretical. Both are judicial in character, but arbitration leaves broader scope for the elements of compromise and adjustment in the decision. One distinction, however, is that judicial settlement is made by an existing bench of judges, whereas arbitration is by judges chosen for the specific case.

By all these means, hundreds of disputes were disposed of, and by 1914 it seemed that the world was strengthening the methods of peaceful settlement.

We cannot leave this period in development of the methods of peace without reference to the long line of American Secretaries of State who so steadily contributed to the road building of peace. The names of James Monroe, John Hay, and Elihu Root especially stand out in the records of the time.

Summary of Peace Movements

Thus, gradually there developed in this period three pacific concepts: first, the establishment of international rules and law by agreement and precedent; second, the development of methods of settling controversies by arbitration and cooling off; third, the development of co-operation in economic and social fields.

But if we examine all these movements, we again find that the use of military force, or threats of its use to keep the peace, dominantly prevailed at least in practice. The Quadruple Alliance, the Triple Alliance, the Entente Cordiale, the balance of power, the Monroe Doctrine—all belong to that category. But proposals of pacific methods of solution or relief of disputes and tensions through morals and reason made the greatest advances in history up to this time. The Holy Alliance; the Concert of Europe; the development of law and international cooperation; disarmament; arbitration and mediation; and change in purpose of diplomacy—all contributed to these strides.

Despite the great efforts of men devoted to peace, the six underlying dynamic forces—ideologies; economic pressures; nationalism; imperialism; militarism; and the complexes of fear, hate, and revenge—had culminated in a gigantic crisis by 1914.

PART II

CHAPTER V

The First World War

HERE AGAIN we are interested not in military history, but in the force's which make for war and peace. Therefore, we do not describe the military campaigns or battles, or the heroism and sacrifice of millions of men whose deeds are the great rays of sunlight in the gigantic tragedy of the first World War.

In this chapter we shall first review the final pressures of the seven dynamic forces which led to this gigantic explosion, then offer some description of the effect of the war upon the dynamic forces themselves, and finally enumerate the expressed peace aims and purposes of the United Nations in seeking victory.

THE FINAL EXPLOSION

Historians will not be able to measure the relative weight of these seven forces in producing this gigantic upheaval until long hence, when they can be examined in the light of all their consequences. But from this distance of a generation we can make some observations upon them.

The superficial causes of the war started from Sarajevo, in June 1914. But the assassination of an archduke could not alone have provoked a world war had it not been for the antecedent development in the dynamic forces which we have outlined in the last chapters. Six out of the seven had risen to pressures beyond the safety valve of the seventh—the will to peace.

It is a matter of speculation whether with more capable or more clear-minded statesmanship, crises could have been allayed and the debacle deferred. It might be said speculatively that had Serbian statesmen quickly realized the heinousness of the crime of Sarajevo and made immediate amends, even though humiliating, had the Russian statesmen not been looking for war as a diversion from domestic troubles, had Germany wished to avert conflict, had Britain taken a positive stand earlier in the crisis, the conflict might have been averted for the moment. In other words, the fundamental pressures of the dynamic forces of explosion were present, but inadequate statesmanship did not recognize them, or failed, or did not wish to allay them. Be that as it may, these evil forces were released, and from releasing them were created more evils, and thus came the first *total* war.

Undoubtedly, even had the incident at Sarajevo been tided over, the pressures had become too great for the explosion to be long deferred without constructive allaying of these forces in Europe. That they were tinder for a match is evident from a short review of them.

IDEOLOGICAL PRESSURES.[1] The pressure of ideological forces—the struggle of men for liberty against subjection

[1]For outline of these forces, see p. 12; 140 years prior to World War I p. 40.

—had become potent in the causes of the war. The march of personal liberty and representative government had raised internal explosions in Russia, Germany, and Austria by demands of their people for more liberty. And liberty had inspired the rising forces of nationalism and demands for independence in the races they held in subjection. The men around the emperors welcomed a diversion of their peoples' minds from the internal pressures of nationalism and liberty over into foreign dangers even if at the moment they did not consciously envisage war.

The importance of the ideological forces in the causes of the war were at the outbreak obscured by the military grouping of nations. The alliance of the representative governments of France and England with Czarist Russia would not indicate a military crusade to impose democracy. Indeed, America was not fully convinced of the ideological purity of the Allies until the collapse of Czarist Russia in March 1917, before we entered the war. Nevertheless, the basic conflict was there. The peoples of the western European nations certainly raised these grounds of antagonism to the Central Empires.

There cannot be the remotest doubt that alarm for the ideals of personal liberty and representative government was the major pressure for the entrance of the United States into the war.

It is true that the unlimited submarine warfare, with its attacks upon American shipping, and the Zimmermann note, with its revelation of German designs, had a crystallizing effect.

No one, however, can read the ideals and aims expressed by President Wilson without accepting the fact that, so far as the United States was concerned, this was dominantly an armed crusade to defeat aggression and to make personal liberty and representative government supreme in the world. These aims were supported by the American people and were quickly coined into popular terms of "war to end war," "to make the world safe for democracy," "to destroy militarism and aggression," "to bring freedom to mankind"—all are ample evidence of the character of the American purpose.

If further proof were needed of our major idealistic purpose, our self-denying ordinances of no annexations of territory and no indemnities amply indicate that there was no imperialism or nationalism behind American purposes. With only a police army, we had no militaristic pressure. We were under no economic pressures of any kind. There was no inherent hate of Germany or Austria. Our declarations that we had no purpose of vengeance or punishment of the enemy peoples further emphasized this. In fact, before 1914 the general feeling throughout the nation was perhaps more friendly to Germany than to Britain. There was no fear of invasion of our continent or loss of our independence. We had no internal pressure of any kind for which politicians needed diversion of public mind to foreign affairs and war. The will to peace ran high among us.

So when we did go to war, it was the most gigantic crusade of all history.

ECONOMIC PRESSURES.[2] The economic pressures of the Industrial Revolution had created great dangers. The push for elbow room and foreign markets, the dependence upon overseas supplies of food and raw materials had created intense rivalries and a consequent growth of

[2]For outline of these pressures, see p. 13; 140 years prior to World War I, p. 44.

huge navies. Everywhere, nations were building barriers around trade and seeking special privilege and advantage. For these reasons the friction between Britain and Germany especially had grown most acute. The push of German capital into the Near East had stirred Russia. Economic pressures had, in fact, risen to the incendiary stage.

NATIONALISM.[3] The accumulated forces of nationalism were tearing at the vitals of the German, Russian, Austrian, and Turkish empires. A dozen races were striving for independence from the old empires. That became evident enough when these old empires later on split into thirteen independent nations by the rebellions of their subject peoples seeking freedom.

IMPERIALISM.[4] The clash of rival imperialisms was clanging with war. And it came, not alone from economic pressures, but from the impulses of national glory and national arrogance. The two rival centers of imperialism, in Russia and in Germany, were constantly at each other's throats, particularly in the Balkans.

MILITARISM.[5] Aggressive militarism was rampant in Russia, Germany and Austria. Their military castes had built mammoth armaments and were on the march for glory. The two huge military alliances themselves invited war. The Triple Alliance of Germany, Austria, and Italy had forced France, out of fear, to join in counteralliance

[3]For outline of this force, see p. 13; 140 years prior to World War I, p. 49.

[4]For outline of this force, see p. 17; 140 years prior to World War I, p. 51.

[5]For outline of this force, see p. 15; 140 years prior to World War I, p. 56.

with Russia. Britain's policy of balance of power had given friendly support to France. The cost of competitive arms rocketed. The annual expenditure on arms in the Western World had increased from about $1,500,000,000 to more than $5,000,000,000 in the five years prior to 1914. It could not go on increasing the numbers and power of men whose mission was fighting without eventually cultivating a fight. This increase itself was an indication of rising pressures.

FEAR, HATE, AND REVENGE.[6] And impelling to the final debacle were fear, hate, and revenge: French and British fear of Germany; German fear of Britain and Russia; Austrian fear and hate of Russia; Russian fear of Germany; French hate and resolve of revenge against Germany; and all the hates of the subject races.

THE WILL TO PEACE.[7] All these pressures were too much to be subdued by the Will to Peace alone. The instruments of the old power diplomacy, the balance of power, the Concert of Europe and even the newer machinery of international law and international co-operation, driven with frantic efforts by the British and French Foreign Ministers, all totally failed to prevent the explosion.

CHANGES IN THE SEVEN DYNAMIC FORCES IMPOSED DURING THE WAR

The seven dynamic forces were certain to be changed by the heat from the furnace of war. Some of these changes developed during the course of the war itself and

[6]For outline of these forces, see p. 19; before World War I, p. 58.

[7]For outline of this force, see p. 20; 140 years prior to World War I, p. 60.

require examination for the effect they had upon the peace conference—and afterwards.

TOTAL WAR. The most vital of these changes came from the development for the first time in history of what was well called "total war."

Sometime after the Franco-Prussian War of the 1870s, the whole character of war had changed. Prior to that, the broad art of war had been about the same for over 300 years. It is true, firearms had been perfected in detail, but methods of military organization, tactics, and strategy were broadly of the same character. Sea power changed little in its relationship to the factors in war.

In those earlier times, armies and navies called out only a fraction of the population. Their support required only another fraction. Thus, there was only a fractional disruption of economic and social life during the war. But the Industrial Revolution, with its mechanical inventions, had given birth to total war. It had perfected ability to produce firearms in far greater volume. Improvements in rail, water, highway, and truck transportation had made it possible to maneuver far larger bodies of men. Thus, during the first World War, armies grew to the total man power which could be spared from production of arms and the minimum supply of necessities to the civil population.

The invention of the gas engine had made possible the truck, the airplane, the submarine, and later the tank. Other inventions had made possible the heavier artillery, the improved machine gun and rifle, and poison gas. These weapons had become not only more hideously destructive but more complicated to make and far more expensive. Thus, huge specialized factories and millions more of mechanics were required to support the larger armies.

And the calling of the maximum man power to the fighting front and the need of maximum supply services for them required, for the first time, total mobilization of the civil population under great compulsions and restrictions imposed by governments. Herein was what amounted to a profound revolution.

Starvation of Nations as a Weapon. As we have said, the huge populations resulting from the Industrial Revolution, such as those of Germany, England, and Japan, had become dependent upon overseas imports for food and raw materials. While to besiege and starve a city is as old as Babylon, never until 1914 had the starvation of whole nations been made so effective by blockade. It was proved that sea power could starve whole empires for food, and all their industries for raw material.

Blockade was now aided by another special phenomenon of total war. That was the rapid degeneration of agriculture. Because of the lack of imported fats and animal feed, great inroads were made into the flocks and herds in order to live. Work stock was used up in war. Fertilizers had to be diverted to explosives. Shortage of labor curtailed planting and harvesting of ground crops. In the enemy countries, these shortages undermined the health and the stability of their children. In the Allied countries, the shortage of shipping and man power had the same effects on agricultural production, but the people secured their marginal needs by imports.

The economic consequences of diversion of normal production to war materials—the diversion of occupation, the displacement of populations, the introduction of women into industry—were on a scale never dreamed of in war before.

And the gigantic sums required to finance all these diversions of economic life to war made huge inflation during the war inevitable.

A New Ideology Is Born. In the end, profound consequences were to come to the whole world from the ideological thinking arising out of the organization of whole peoples for total war.

Representative government itself contributed to the beginnings of a malevolent and hostile ideology. In order to mobilize the whole energies of their peoples, all governments at war had to plan and enforce production and to divert men and material to war purposes. They were compelled to restrict production for civilian purposes. Governments had to operate industry and dictate to business, labor, and agriculture. And where men claimed old personal rights, they had to be coerced. All this was as much needed in the countries of liberty as in those accustomed to subjection. Thus, representative government everywhere surrendered economic and personal freedom to the state that they might win the war. Government management of economic life during the war was assisted greatly by the fact that altruism and patriotism replaced self-interest as the basis of economic production and service. But the world at that spot laid the foundations of "managed economy," and thus the economics of a new ideology —Fascism.

The Corruption of Intellectual and Spiritual Freedom. The desperations of total war gave birth to other inroads upon liberty in the democracies themselves.

Truth proved to be the first fatality of war. Total war required government-organized propaganda. And propaganda is, at best, only part truth. The atrocities and wickedness of the enemy must be constantly illustrated. The hates of the people at home, their courage and their aspirations could not be allowed to lag in the face of suffering and reverses. Neutrals must be influenced to keep neutral or to help. The enemy had to be misled. All governments engaged in these processes without any moral restraint. Telling lies was saving the lives of sons. It was further justified among the representative governments on the ground that victory must be had, for defeat in total war meant defeat of liberty itself.

And total war bred total intolerance. National unity was essential in the face of total national danger. But impatience at discussion rose to rabid intolerance, even at discussion of constructive character. There was no need for government in the democracies to suppress free speech. The crowd howled it down. And government-inspired propaganda could and did injure many of its own citizens, no matter how pure their patriotism.

Total war created more hideous brutalities than had any war since the Middle Ages. Total war was a war of civilian effort against civilian effort as well as of armies against armies. Therefore, to dislocate civilian activities on the enemy side became a part of military action. Thus, it became also a war of armies against civilians. No longer was there chivalry of armed men for women and children. Starvation of nations brought not only agony to civilians, but stunting of their children and decimation of millions from inevitable pestilence. Terrorization of civilians was organized as an act of war. Towns were burned by the Germans as warnings, and innocent hostages were mowed down by machine guns. Airplanes and zeppelins were used to drop iron and fire upon helpless civilians, to burn their homes and their cities. Civilian sailors were sunk by submarines without a chance of survival.

One bright spot in all this welter of brutality was the efforts of people of good will to alleviate suffering. The Commission for Relief in Belgium, through consent of both sides, preserved the lives of 10,000,000 invaded and blockaded people over the period of four years. During and after the war, the American Red Cross, the Friends' Service Committee, and other organizations played a splendid role in alleviating the sufferings of war.

THE GROWTH OF HATE. And total war, from the brutalities to civilians, produced total hate and total demand for revenge. Hate enveloped the mind of every man, woman, and child. It was not directed solely to the enemy leaders, but to every individual in enemy countries. Soldiers fighting at the front had far less hate than civilians.

During 1916 there came a moment when reason said there should be a negotiated peace. The Central Powers might thus have avoided collapse into chaos. The Allies stood to gain more substantial and lasting advantages. President Wilson tried to initiate such a peace. There is little doubt that most of the European statesmen on both sides recognized the desirability of such a peace and would have been glad to consider it. But the peoples on both sides had been aroused to such a pitch of anger and hate that they would have overthrown any statesman who manifested a readiness to consider a negotiated peace. Total war, flogged on by the propaganda of hate, had no terminal short of the surrender of one side or the other through defeat or exhaustion. And in that respect the victor was but one lap ahead of the vanquished.

War Aims. As the war moved on, there were profound changes at least in its aims. These changes were in considerable part due to the entrance of America and the emphasis given to ideological purpose.

Before the war was ended by the Armistice, President Wilson had repeatedly expressed America's aspirations in the aims and principles of the peace to come. Because of their profound effect upon ending the war and upon the peacemaking, we must examine them closely.

At the end of this chapter we have grouped his aims and proposals on the basis of their relation to the seven forces: ideological; economic; nationalistic; imperialistic; militaristic; the complexes of fear, hate, and revenge; and the yearning for lasting peace.

The Armistice. During the year before the Armistice, Mr. Wilson had enumerated these aims in his Fourteen Points, and later extended them to twenty-five points in the subsequent addresses covering the basis of peace, which we give at the end of the chapter. The moral, economic, and military strength of the United States had swung the balance over to victory. The Allies, bled white by their efforts, had arrived at a stalemate. But for the United States, the Allies could not have attained victory. The American people never organized, co-operated, or sacrificed more efficiently in their national history, nor did their sons ever rise to greater heights of discipline and valor. Nor did American military leadership ever rise to greater heights than under General Pershing and Admirals Benson, Pratt, and Sims.

During the month of October 1918, at Germany's request, Mr. Wilson negotiated the basis of the Armistice on behalf of all the Allies. That basis was Germany's specific acceptance of the Fourteen Points and the "subsequent addresses." But before closing the agreement with Germany, the President submitted the entire proposals to the Allied Powers and received their formal acceptance except for one point—the freedom of the seas.

With these ideas and ideals established, the war was won and the Armistice signed. It provided for the complete surrender of the arms of Germany, and her retreat into her own borders. A peace was to be negotiated later, and the Armistice promised that food would be provided in the meantime.

The destruction of life and property was unparalleled in its proportions to any previous war in history, except perhaps the Thirty Years' War. Government debts of somewhere near $250,000,000,000 were piled up. Huge numbers of ships, factories, homes were destroyed. Some 10,000,000 men were killed or maimed, probably 10,000,000 civilians died of starvation or disease resulting from the war. And 350,000,000 people were left disastrously short of food, heat and clothing. The third and fourth Horsemen of the Apocalypse—Famine and Pestilence—were the rulers of men. And a fifth Horseman was to appear—Revolution.

Declared War Aims

For later reference, we have here paralleled President Wilson's declarations with those on the present war made thus far by President Roosevelt.

Ideological Aims

WILSON

The soldiers at the front . . . They are crusaders . . . are giving their lives, that homes everywhere . . . may be kept sacred and safe and men everywhere be free as they insist upon being free.

Sept. 1, 1918

Longing of the oppressed . . . to hear something like the "Battle Hymn of the Republic"; to hear the feet of the great hosts of liberty going to set them free, to set their minds free, set their lives free, set their children free. . . .

May 18, 1918

It is our inestimable privilege . . . to make not only the liberties of America secure but the liberties of every other people as well. . . .

We have heard and watched the struggle for self-government spread and triumph among many peoples. We have come to regard the right to political liberty as the common right of humankind. Year after year . . . we have continued to re-

ROOSEVELT

In the future days which we seek to make secure, we look forward to a world founded upon four essential freedoms.

The first is freedom of speech and expression—everywhere in the world.

The second is freedom of every person to worship God in his own way—everywhere in the world.

The third is freedom from want, which translated into world terms means economic understandings which will secure to every nation a healthy peacetime life for its inhabitants—everywhere in the world.

The fourth is freedom from fear, which translated into world terms means reduction of armaments to such a point and in such thorough fashion that no nation will be in position to commit an act of physical aggression against any neighbor—anywhere in the world.

Jan. 7, 1941

We will accept only a world consecrated to freedom of speech and expression—freedom of every person to worship God

WILSON

joice in the peaceful increase of freedom and democracy throughout the world. . . . We are confronted with a menace which endangers everything that we have won and the world has won. . . . In all its old insolence, with all its ancient cruelty and injustice, military autocracy has again armed itself against the pacific hopes of men. . . .

We are face to face with the necessity of asserting anew the fundamental right of free men to make their own laws, choose their own allegiance, or else permit humanity to become the victim of a ruthless ambition that is determined to destroy what it cannot master. . . . The past and present are in deadly struggle. . . .

What we seek is the reign of law based upon the consent of the governed and sustained by the organized opinion of mankind. I ask you, fellow citizens, to unite with them in making this our Independence Day the first that shall be consecrated to a declaration of independence for all the peoples of the world.

July 4, 1918

ROOSEVELT

in his own way—freedom from want and freedom from terror.

May 28, 1941

The essence of our struggle is that men shall be free.

Nov. 6, 1941

There must be no place in the postwar world for special privilege, either for individuals or nations.

Nov. 6, 1941

This duty we owe . . . is to make the world a place where freedom can live and grow into the ages.

Nov. 6, 1941

We are fighting today for security, for progress, and for peace, not only for ourselves but for all men, not only for one generation but for all generations. We are fighting to cleanse the world of ancient evils, ancient ills . . .

Jan. 6, 1942

We are fighting, as our fathers have fought, to uphold the doctrine that all men are equal in the sight of God. Those on the other side are striving

WILSON

What is the war for? . . . It is a war of emancipation. Not until it is won can men anywhere live free from constant fear or breathe freely while they go about their daily tasks and know that governments are their servants not their masters. . . .

Sept. 1, 1918

What we are striving for is a new international order based upon broad and universal principles of right and justice, no mere peace of shreds and patches.

Feb. 11, 1918

Our desire for a new international order under which reason and justice and common interest of mankind . . . shall prevail . . . without that new order the world will be without peace.

Feb. 11, 1918

Our passion for justice and self-government is no mere passion which once set in motion must be satisfied.

Feb. 11, 1918

ROOSEVELT

to destroy this deep belief and to create a world in their own image—a world of tyranny and cruelty and serfdom.

Jan. 6, 1942

The present great struggle has taught us increasingly that freedom of person and security of property anywhere in the world depend upon the security of the rights and obligations of liberty and justice everywhere in the world.

Feb. 24, 1942

The First World War

Economic Aims

WILSON

The removal as far as possible of all economic barriers and the establishment of equality of trade condition among all nations consenting to the peace and associating themselves for its maintenance.

Jan. 31, 1918

There can be no special selfish economic combinations within the League . . . no economic boycott or exclusion . . . except by the League.

Sept. 27, 1918

[Mr. Wilson's specific labor aims were expressed in the creation of the International Labor Office.]

Absolute freedom of navigation upon the seas outside territorial waters (except where closed by international agreement).

Jan. 8, 1918

ROOSEVELT

They desire to bring about the fullest collaboration between all nations in the economic field with the object of improved labor standards, economic advancement, and social security.

Churchill-Roosevelt, Aug. 13, 1941

They will endeavor with due respect for existing obligations to further the enjoyment by all states, great and small, victor and vanquished, of access on equal terms to the trade and to the raw material of the world which are needed for their economic prosperity.

Churchill-Roosevelt, Aug. 13, 1941

Such a peace should enable men to traverse the high seas and oceans without hindrance.

Churchill-Roosevelt, Aug. 13, 1941

. . . No nation has the right to make the broad oceans of the world at great distances from the actual theater of land war unsafe for the commerce of others.

Sept. 11, 1941

SELF-DETERMINATION AND NATIONALISM

WILSON

. . . National aspirations must be respected; peoples may now be dominated and governed only by their consent. "Self-determination" is not mere phrase. It is an imperative principle of action. . . .

Feb. 11, 1918

Satisfaction of those deep-seated longings of oppressed . . . and enslaved peoples.

Sept. 27, 1918

Peoples are not to be handed about from one sovereignty to another by an international conference.

. . . Peoples and provinces are not to be bartered about from sovereignty to sovereignty as if they were mere chattels and pawns in a game. . . . Every territorial settlement involved in this war must be made in the interest of the populations concerned and not . . . adjustment or compromise of claims among rival states. . . .

Feb. 11, 1918

[President Wilson, in the Fourteen Points, proposed

ROOSEVELT

They respect the right of all peoples to choose the form of government under which they will live.

Churchill-Roosevelt, Aug. 13, 1941

They desire to see no territorial changes that do not accord with the freely expressed wishes of the people concerned.

Churchill-Roosevelt, Aug. 13, 1941

They wish to see sovereign rights and self-government restored to those who have been forcibly deprived of them.

Churchill-Roosevelt, Aug. 13, 1941

We of the United Nations are agreed on certain broad principles in the kind of peace we seek . . . disarmament of aggressors, self-determination of nations and peoples. . . .

Feb. 24, 1942

WILSON

specifically the restoration of Belgium, Alsace-Lorraine, Rumania, Montenegro, Poland; the creation of Czechoslovakia, Yugoslavia; the union of the Italian-speaking peoples; the autonomy or freedom of non-Turkish races (Armenians, Arabs, Syrians, Palestine); and the freedom of the Dardanelles.]

Jan. 8, 1918 and
Oct. 26, 1918

[Russia] an unhampered and unembarrassed opportunity for the independent determination of her own political development . . . a sincere welcome into the society of free nations under institutions of her own choosing. . . .

Jan. 8, 1918

No Imperialism

WILSON

There shall be no annexation. . . .

Feb. 11, 1918

Free, open-minded, and absolutely impartial adjustment of all colonial claims . . . based

ROOSEVELT

Their countries seek no aggrandizement, territorial or other.

Churchill-Roosevelt,
Aug. 13, 1941

WILSON

upon the interests of the population concerned. . . .

Jan. 8, 1918

"German colonies should be declared the common property of the League and administered by small nations."

Dec. 12, 1918[8]

Destruction of Militarism

WILSON

The day of conquest and aggrandizement has gone by.

Jan. 8, 1918

But it is necessary we must frankly say, and necessary as a preliminary to any intelligent dealings with her [Germany] on our part that we should know whom her spokesman speak for when they speak to us, whether for the Reichstag majority or for the Military Party and those men whose creed is imperial domination.

Jan. 8, 1918

. . . She [the United States] entered this war because she

ROOSEVELT

After the final destruction of the Nazi tyranny. . . .

Churchill-Roosevelt,
Aug. 13, 1941

Since no future peace can be maintained if land, sea, or air armaments continue to be employed by nations which threaten aggression outside their frontiers, they believe pending the establishment of a wider and permanent system of general security that the disarmament of such nations is essential. They will likewise aid and encourage all other practicable measures which will lighten for

[8]Ray Stannard Baker, *Woodrow Wilson and World Settlement,* Doubleday, Page, Vol. I, p. 19.

WILSON

was made a partner . . . in the sufferings and indignities inflicted by the military masters of Germany against the peace and security of mankind.

Feb. 11, 1918

Not . . . even the great game now forever discredited of the balance of power.

Feb. 11, 1918

. . . These great ends cannot be achieved by debating and seeking to reconcile . . . their projects of balances of power and of national opportunity.

July 4, 1918

We know that there cannot be another balance of power. That has been tried and found wanting.

Dec. 2, 1918

Special alliances and economic rivalries and hostilities have been the prolific source in the modern world of the plans and passions that produce war. It would be an . . . insecure peace that did not exclude them in definite and binding terms. . . .

There can be no league or alliance or special covenants and

ROOSEVELT

peace-loving peoples the crushing burdens of armaments.

Churchill-Roosevelt,
Aug. 13, 1941

We of the United Nations are agreed on certain broad principles in the kind of peace we seek . . . disarmament of aggressors. . . .

Feb. 24, 1942

WILSON

understandings with the general and common family of the League of Nations.

Sept. 27, 1918

Adequate guarantees given and taken that national armaments will be reduced to the lowest point consistent with domestic safety.

Jan. 8, 1918

To Allay Hate, Fear and Revenge

WILSON

The war shall not end in vindictive action of any kind; that no nation or people shall be robbed or punished because irresponsible rulers of a single country have themselves done a deep and abominable wrong.

Dec. 4, 1917

We wish her [Germany] only to accept a place of equality among the peoples of the world . . . instead of a place of mastery.

Jan. 8, 1918

I call you to witness, my fellow countrymen, that at no stage of this terrible busi-

ROOSEVELT

After the final destruction of the Nazi tyranny they hope to see established a peace which will afford all nations the means of dwelling in safety within their own boundaries and which will afford assurance that all men may live out their lives in freedom from fear and want.

Churchill-Roosevelt, Aug. 13, 1941

We are now in the midst of a war, not for conquest, not for vengeance, but for a world in which this nation and all this nation represents will be safe for our children.

Dec. 9, 1941

WILSON

ness have I judged the purposes of Germany intemperately. I should be ashamed, in the presence of affairs so grave, so fraught with the destinies of mankind throughout the world, to speak with truculence, to use the weak language of hatred or vindictive purpose.

April 6, 1918

There shall be no . . . contributions, no punitive damages.

Feb. 11, 1918

The settlement of every question whether of territory, of sovereignty or economic arrangement, or of political relationship upon the basis of free acceptance of that settlement by the people immediately concerned and not on the basis of the material advantage of any other nation. . . .

July 4, 1918

The impartial justice meted out must involve no discrimination between those to whom we wish to be just and those to whom we do not wish to be just.

Sept. 27, 1918

WILSON

It is the principle of justice to all peoples and nationalities and their right to live on equal terms of liberty and safety with one another whether they be weak or strong.

Jan. 8, 1918

THE WILL TO PEACE

WILSON

A general association of nations must be formed under specific covenants for the purpose of affording mutual guarantees of political independence and territorial integrity to great and small states alike.

Jan. 8, 1918

The indispensable instrumentality is a League of Nations . . . without such an instrumentality by which the peace of the world can be guaranteed peace will rest in part upon the word of outlaws . . . the constitution of the League of Nations . . . must be . . . the most essential part of the peace settlement itself.

Sept. 27, 1918

Open covenants of peace openly arrived at—diplomacy always frankly in public view.

Jan. 8, 1918

CHAPTER VI

The Seven Dynamic Forces during the Armistice and Peacemaking 1918–19

JUST AS NEITHER sin nor goodness can be abolished from the world, the seven dynamic forces that make for peace and war cannot be eliminated. The real problem before the peace conference was to allay those forces that made for war and to strengthen those which made for peace.

Some were altered during the progress of the war. Some were altered as a consequence of the war. But they were all in action the day after the Armistice, and, for that matter, always will be this side of the millennium. And statesmen are too often dominated by the less peaceful ones.

It is not our purpose to describe the drama of peace negotiations, the gilded halls, the pomp and circumstance surrounding these scores of nations with their celebrated representatives and their protocols of politeness. We are interested in the grim unseen forces which haunted the halls of peace and shaped the coming world.

After the Armistice, the American peace argosy, with President Wilson on board, sailed from America, confident that victory had now brought the opportunity to build a new order of "freedom to mankind," "based upon the broad and universal principles of justice" in which "reason and justice and the common interest of mankind shall prevail," a "lasting peace"—not "a mere peace of shreds and patches," in which economic wrong, selfish nationality, imperialism, militarism, hate, revenge, and fear should be forever buried in the new order.

Americans generally failed to realize how far, in our 300 years of separation, our outlook, our political and social ideas and ideals had grown apart from the practical methods and problems of Europe. This is not said in contention that our ideals were superior. It is merely an indication of a development which was to have a profound influence upon events.

Our freedom from age-old hate of our neighbors, our freedom from fears of invasion, our centuries of national safety, our abundant resources, our ease of living, and the blessings of liberty allowed us to indulge in the luxury of concepts wholly different from those of Europe. Having made a fresh and independent start in the New World, our concepts of democracy had grown apart from the class stratifications and class barriers and class governments of democratic Europe. We had grown far apart in our thinking.

Our warm hopes met at once the freezing blasts of centuries of European mores. To them we were bearers of impractical and strange notions for dealing with their problems. Our ideas clashed against the backgrounds of their realistic necessities. Our representatives had little appreciation of the subtle forces moving in these scores of nations and of the genuine obstacles to the acceptance of some of our ideas.

Our European Allies lived in a grimly practical world in which they believed the tried principles of old power diplomacy afforded the only way to deal adequately with the forces of economic nationalism, economic necessity, imperialism, age-old hates, punishment, revenge, and general disorder. Their nations had lived amid a struggle for existence where every proposal was examined in the cold light of national advantage.

To handle this new phenomenon from the Western World, they summoned the skilled hands of the old diplomacy. It was the process with which over the centuries they had dealt with a hundred European crises. Their representatives belonged to classes and schools which had been born to this profession. They practiced the art with skill that comes from centuries of inheritance and training. Their formulae were seasoned in the history of Europe. The shades of Machiavelli, Marlborough, Pitt, Castlereagh, Talleyrand were all about in their spiritual descendants. To them, this was simply another crisis and no crusade of idealists. They were not impressed—below the skin at least.

The proofs of this lie not only in the incidents and outcome of the peacemaking, but in the official actions and the subsequent ample writings of the European statesmen on the Allied side. They are now the open book of history and need no specific reference.

Here was the greatest chance of all history for statesmen to dominate the evil dynamic forces, but statesmanship ignored them or proved unequal to the task. However, in all this we must recognize the desperation of the situation, the wholly different points of view and ideals of nations separated by centuries of different development and environment.

The misfortune of the world is that, instead of the destructive dynamic forces being allayed, they were given new impulses which plunged the world into World War II.

But American ideals, so well formulated by President Wilson, were not without some victories. Their very vitality carried some of them at least into temporary acceptance.

Here we have the advantage of hindsight and here we may again examine the problem, not in a spirit of captious criticism, but in a desire to extract what lessons we can. Man is not blessed with as much foresight as he is with the ability of availing himself of his hard experience.

The Ideologies[1]

The outstanding immediate result of the war was the advance of representative government. Indeed, this victory came before the peacemakers could meet. It had only to confirm accomplished facts.

The ideals of representative government and of personal and national liberty, so much emphasized by America, had stimulated democratic revolutions which, at the Armistice, swept over the enemy states up to the Russian border. President Wilson's insistence upon "self-determination" and the right of races to their own self-government had started a potent ferment long before the Armistice. A dozen races had completed their independence before the peace conference assembled.

[1]For outline of these pressures, see p. 12; before World War I, p. 40; in World War I, p. 82.

Revolutions in old enemy states installed representative government in full. Long before the war, the great mass of common people in the enemy areas were already fertilized by its preachments. Now their own struggles to attain personal liberty installed at least the forms of representative government. Germany, Hungary, Austria, dismissed the last shreds of despotism. Unfortunately, they went too far and nullified much of the good that might have been achieved by more moderate measures. The revolution was no doubt made easier by the acquiescence of the warrior classes, hoping for softer terms in defeat. But, nevertheless, the men who came to the top in this revolution were for the most part genuinely liberal and wanted fervently to make democracy work. They especially wanted to turn Germany's face from militarism; they hoped to direct her toward social and economic advancement. They wanted her to co-operate with the other representative governments.

The liberated peoples of Finland, Latvia, Estonia, Lithuania, Poland, Czechoslovakia, Rumania, Croatia, Serbia, Slovenia all adopted personal liberty and representative government as the foundation of national life. Britain, France, Italy, Belgium, Sweden, Norway, Holland, Denmark, Switzerland, and Greece had long since adopted various liberal governmental forms.

Thus, representative government had spread over the whole of Europe up to the Russian frontier. It seemed that the freedom of men had triumphed over almost all the civilized world. It seemed that the World War was but a triumphant incident in the glorious march of mankind toward freedom.

To the Americans, this was not only a crowning success in their purpose, but it was their policy in peacemaking to sustain these representative governments. And here came the most severe clash of American concepts with the Allies and old diplomacy. In the roots of what was done about this problem lay much of the woe to come to the world.

To thoughtful Americans the cornerstone of the edifice of lasting peace after Versailles was not the League of Nations. The real hope lay in representative government. That in itself signified the overthrow of the spirits of aggression, autocracy, militarism, the Junker landlord castes, the remnants of feudalism, the re-establishment of the rights of men as against slavery to state and class. It was the American belief that these newly freed peoples, if able to act, would refuse to stand for militarism and the burdens of aggressive arms or to vote themselves into war—except against attack. But their ability to assert themselves in this peaceful sense depended upon growth of the tender plants of representative government and personal liberty which had sprung up with the Armistice in the old militaristic areas. A chief purpose of the League, as we saw it then, was to safeguard the growth of these forces of freedom.

Yet subsequent revolt from these forces was in part born in the peace treaty itself. We discuss elsewhere the question of punishment of the enemy states. The treaty certainly leaned to the side of hate, fear, and revenge rather than toward statesmanship. The real problem was not one of abstract justice. Justice could never liquidate the wrongs which the ruling caste of Prussia had done the world. The practical fact was that the evil should have been charged to their leaders, as had been promised, and the people should have been given a chance.

Many actions by the Allied governments during the

Armistice and in the peace treaty weakened the liberal movement in the enemy states. The German people unquestionably believed they had surrendered upon the basis of the Wilson points. That these points were not applied to Germany very exhaustively is manifest. Whether Germany would have surrendered anyway, or whether she kept her own promises, is not to the point. The point is in the beliefs and emotions of a whole nation.

The leaders of Germany bore a heavy weight of responsibility for the origin and conduct of the war. Their armies had spread grief and suffering and devastation far and wide. No amount of punishment could have been devised to do full justice for the crimes and brutality of those four years. Nothing we may say in criticism of the course followed by the victors in dealing with Germany can soften the judgment of the behavior of her war leaders. But entirely aside from the question of their responsibility, we have an unfortunate record of actions which undermined the edifice of peace while it was being built.

One of the most humiliating of all actions to the Germans was the requirement that the democratic regime sign a war-guilt clause—a confession that the whole nation was guilty of causing the war. This did not bother the militarists—they all escaped—but the millions who had no voice on the war did object, and the foundation was laid for their later support of the militarists in wiping out this stain. The avowal of guilt, signed under duress, brought us no advantage, but, on the other hand, gave successive German agitators a ready-made grievance to exploit.

Another futile and even wicked thrust of Allied militarism and punishment was continuing the food blockade against Germany after the Armistice on November 11,

1918. The provisions of the Armistice promised food, but no food was allowed in until nearly five months later, in the latter part of March 1919. And expanding the blockade after the Armistice, by the British and French fleets to the Baltic fisheries, made it worse. All this is a black chapter in human history for which no blame attaches to the American people. Our representatives fought against this action daily and hourly during the entire period, and that its ultimate relaxation before peace was signed was due to American insistence. We did have the strong support of certain liberal-minded Englishmen, such as Lord Robert Cecil and Lord Eustace Percy. The suffering of the people in the enemy states after November 11 under the continued blockade was far more acute than that prior to the Armistice. With revolution and weakened government the old distribution and rationing machinery greatly deteriorated. Between farmers hoarding and the richer people bootlegging, a blow came to the children of Germany which subsequent large-scale American charity was not able to remedy.

A further action which was to carry seeds of destruction into the new regime in Germany was the absurd levying of indemnities or "reparations" of $40,000,000,000 upon a people that even under no concept of economic slavery could deliver half the interest on that sum in foreign exchange. Under the terms of the treaty, the Germans were stripped of ships, of much of their private property in foreign lands and even at home. The reparations in kind, chiefly coal from the New Reich and the separation of coal districts, undermined her industrial strength. Just or unjust, wise or unwise, the consequence of these things was to destroy hope and incentive, constantly upset stability, and deter economic recuperation of the world. The whole was punishment for original sin rather than reparation.

The separation of fragments of the German race by Danzig and the Polish Corridor, by territorial changes, and by the prohibition of union with Austria were more punishment than weakening of Germany. Altogether, it decreased Germany's possible population by about 10 per cent. Likewise, the same sort of action toward Hungary, Austria, and Bulgaria sowed dragon's teeth for the future.

It can be said here, and with emphasis, that it was not the fault of Americans that brought these things about. Nor should the statesmen of the Allies be judged too summarily, for there were many desperate forces in operation which often dominated their actions. Our purpose is not to accuse or blame. It is to diagnose.

The freedom of men is again the American purpose in war. If we still hold that it is the cornerstone of a future and lasting peace, we shall need to study all these lessons again.

Economic Pressures[2]

We are not at this point concerned with the economic consequences of the war itself so much as with the pressures which surrounded the peace conference and which were created by the making of peace. Howling storms of economic demoralization surrounded the peace conference with shrill winds crying, "Hurry, hurry, or we perish."

The whole area of the four old empires—Russia, Germany, Austria, and Turkey—was economically exhausted. Italy and France were only one lap behind. Even England

[2]For outline of these forces, see p. 13; before World War I, p. 44; in World War I, p. 84.

was dependent upon the United States for food credits on which to live. The European degeneration in agriculture, with its inevitable famine, demanded relief. The whole of 350,000,000 people were either dangerously short of food or starving. And they had to have food at once or the remnants of civilization would collapse in anarchy or would yield to the seductive call of Communism, now organized and spreading from Russia, subsidized by captured Russian gold. The 200,000,000 people between Russia and the Hindenburg Line had scarcely seen new clothing for four years. They were ragged, tattered, and cold. Then the fourth of the Four Horsemen appeared—Pestilence.

With the Armistice, two new factors made the situation of all these peoples worse than during the war itself. With defeat, the sweep of revolution and the emergence of the thirteen independent nations from disintegration of the four old empires, the wartime controls and restraints collapsed. As mentioned before, the rationing systems of food, clothing, and coal broke down with the removal of the iron hand of military government. Farmers and villagers hoarded what food there was away from the cities.

The economic recasting done by self-determination added another confusion. Each of the thirteen new governments which evolved from the four old empires at once seized all the railway rolling stock and canal boats they could lay hands on. Out of their fears, their hates, their jealousies, and their bad-neighbor policies, they would not allow trains to pass their borders. The railway systems which before the Armistice had fitted the economic life of the old empires were thus broken into fragments. The currencies of the old empires disintegrated and the new states had little security upon which to re-establish them or credits for purchases outside their borders. Thus, the transportation and exchange of goods between surplus areas within Europe were stopped. Coal supplies were inadequate for the minimum of municipal necessities. Hundreds of millions of people in the midst of winter were without heat and light as well as food. Industry was paralyzed; from fifteen to twenty million workmen were unemployed and on public doles.

And add to this the fact that the officials of every one of these new states were for the most part without experience in government. They were nearly all revolutionaries, burning with zeal for the New Order and world politics and so engrossed in that zeal that they had little time or thought for keeping the machinery of everyday life in motion.

The Americans, having the only substantial resources left, and being trusted everywhere as politically disinterested, assumed the burden of finding food; co-ordinating railway, canal, transportation and communication facilities; rehabilitating coal production; improvising credits and currency; organizing new exchange and new systems of rationing supplies; and fighting pestilence. It was not alone a job of saving hundreds of millions from starvation, cold, and disease. It was the job of building stability in government, defeating anarchy and Communism, in order that foundations for any sort of peace could be built. And it was a job of restoring spirit and faith in peoples.

And America did it by the sacrifice of billions of dollars in charity and bad credits, by the distribution of thirty million tons of food, scraped from all parts of the world, by furnishing a dozen governments with expert technical guidance in mobilizing their internal energies to salvation.

Our second intervention in Europe in the name of humanity immediately after the Armistice saved Europe from another collapse such as that after the Thirty Years' War, when it was said a third of the people in Europe had died.

All these economic pressures called for haste in peacemaking. Haste that industry, credit, foreign exchange, and stability might be restored, and haste from fear of impending collapse.

The economic consequences of the peace were not gentle rain on either the just or the unjust. President Wilson had originally denounced all "indemnities or punitive damages," but under the term "reparations" they came into full blossom. There can be no doubt of the ghastly injury the Allies had suffered and the propriety of the old enemies' paying everything within their capacity. The practical question that arose was to assess reparations in such amounts as would not create despair and repudiation or undermine the economy of the enemy states so as to decrease the payments themselves. "You cannot have reparations and revenge at the same time" was the attitude of the Americans. Our delegation wanted to assess a definite annual sum over a limited period of years which would be within the capacity to pay, and by limiting the term, would give hope of eventual release. They also protested at the seizure of private property of enemy citizens all over the world without compensation. But the Allied purpose, particularly that of the French Government, was to devitalize Germany with economic anemia. The preposterous sums levied in the treaty at once started forces that ended by bringing economic degeneration to the world. And from this collapse came a large part of the forces which created Hitler.

The economic systems of the old empires had been integrated over long periods, and their dissolution into a multitude of new states all afire with nationalism played havoc with production and the channels of distribution. Much of this should have been remedied by the peace treaties, but it was not done.

Any American hopes for the reduction of trade barriers were thwarted by the independent action of every new government in Europe at once raising tariffs and setting up special trade agreements partly for political purposes and without even consulting the peacemakers.

In no single case were the prewar economic strains or the strains from the war itself eased by the treaty. They were violently increased.

NATIONALISM[3]

A new and vigorous nationalism blew full blast through every anteroom, every committee room, every conference, every action. The racial fevers of the Allies had been stirred to white heat by the war. And it was even more violent in the liberated nations.

In the Armistice period and under their proclaimed right of self-determination, the oppressed races—the Finns, the Estonians, the Latvians, the Lithuanians, the Poles, the Czechs, the Slovaks, the Croats, the Serbs, the Slovenes, the Armenians, the Georgians, the Azerbaijanese, and the Arabs—all declared their independence. The exiled governments of Belgium, Serbia, Ru-

[3]For outline of this force, see p. 13; before World War I, p. 49; during World War I, p. 85.

mania, and Greece returned to their plundered hearths.

There is no hard and fast line where advantageous development of national spirit ends and selfish destructive nationalism begins. Certain it is that at once every one of these new governments organized an army. They occupied the utmost boundaries that they could secure. They fell into a multitude of conflicts among themselves over how far their racial or historic or economic boundaries should extend. Thus the nations and boundaries of Europe were mainly determined before the peace conference could even convene. Many territorial and other enormities, for which the peace conference has been blamed, were committed before it began—and in some cases against its wishes.

Each country, except the enemy states, sent delegates to Paris at once, not only to secure recognition of their newborn independence, but to oppose the claims of their rivals and to take part in the peacemaking. At once they formed combinations among themselves or adhered as satellites to some major power to influence the decisions of the conference. And they absorbed much of the time and vitality of the conference in their problems.

Just as sure as fate, that will happen again at the next peace. For again, we have quite properly proclaimed the right of peoples to freedom, to self-determination, and self-government. But these concepts are the very fires of nationalism, and these nationalistic forces, with their interests and influences, will again bring their problems for settlement to the confusion of the peacemakers if they are not well prepared and united in advance.

Some of these countries are active through their "free governments" in exile, contributing troops, merchant shipping, and colonial resources to the Allied cause. They will demand repayment in the form of restoration of their national existence and the reconstitution of their boundaries.

IMPERIALISM[4]

Imperialism, which was laid out in death by the American peace aims, had even a rebirth. It not alone had the usual appetites, inherited from the Babylonians, Assyrians, Egyptians, Persians, or some other ancient breed, for territory, exploitation, expression of national growth and glory to returning statesmen, but it also had another impulse. The losses of the war were so high that real economic reparations could come to the Allies only by taking Germany's and Turkey's territorial possessions.

It may be said at once that hopes of indemnities and reparations from impoverished, defeated nations have always proved a delusion. Consequential economic compensation for war is to be found only in the form of territories and peoples to exploit. Whatever its form may be, with the impoverishment of the victors and with their blood shed to protect life and living for other nations, and with many backward races incapable of maintaining self-government, the pressures are to get compensations in exploitation in some fashion.

Under the mandate system, set up in the peace treaty, the British Empire grew by 1,607,053 square miles with 35,000,000 inhabitants; the French Empire gained 402,392 square miles with 4,000,000 inhabitants; the Belgian Empire got 53,000 square miles with 3,387,000 inhabitants; the Japanese Empire was awarded 833 square miles of islands with 113,154 inhabitants. Italy got no mandates. America got nothing—and wanted nothing.

[4]For outline of this force, see p. 17; 140 years prior to World War I, p. 51; in World War I, p. 85.

These areas contained valuable raw materials and markets. They gave valuable outposts for land, air, and naval forces. They certainly stripped Germany from a world empire down to a local state, but they sowed more dragon's teeth. For one thing, they practically gave to Japan the strategic Pacific islands north of the equator that had belonged to Germany. The use made of these islands since was hardly that envisaged by the mandate. For instead of keeping them unarmed, as the mandates required, they were equipped to serve as the naval and air bases from which America is now being attacked.

MILITARISM[5]

The Armistice terms were designed to expunge the force of militarism from the world. German, Austrian, Hungarian, and Bulgarian weapons were taken and destroyed. Germany was disarmed to 100,000 men with no planes, no heavy guns, no tanks, and but few warships. The other enemy nations were allowed but scraps of armies. Herein the peace treaty made a start toward achievement.

But one fatal mistake was made. The old warrior caste was allowed to organize and command the 100,000. Thus they were able to provide for the survival of their class. Under this cover they carried on the tradition of militarism in all its worst forms. They carried on a continuous conspiracy against the peace of the world. It is to them that punishment should have been applied, rather than to the mass of the people.

The treaty provided also for disarmament of all Allied

[5]For outline of this force, see p. 15; 140 years prior to World War I, p. 56; in World War I, p. 85.

nations by conference later on. This deferment was one of the greatest of all treaty mistakes. It should have been done on the spot. General Bliss, the military member of the American delegation, recommended drastic measures of general reduction of armaments to levels essential for internal security. In a letter to the Secretary of War, written from the peace conference, he made this comment:

> Judging from the spirit which seems more and more to dominate our European Allies, I am beginning to despair that the war will accomplish much more than the abolition of *German* militarism while leaving *European* militarism as rampant as ever.

We shall deal with this more fully later on.

Fear, Hate, and Revenge[6]

The evil spirits of fear, hate, and revenge never did more destruction to civilization than at the Paris Conference. They will certainly rise again. As we have said, total war is war on civilians. It is war on women and children. Among our allies, not only had the best of their races been killed upon the field of battle, but their homes had been destroyed, their women and children had been ruthlessly killed from the sky, they had been deprived of food, their sailors had been drowned without mercy, and their peoples had been impoverished for years to come. Total war sank deep its sufferings and hates into every cottage and fireside, arousing a resentment unknown under the older forms of war.

[6]For outline of these forces, see p. 19; 140 years prior to World War I, p. 58; in World War I, p. 86.

Moreover, the French had suffered two invasions from Germany in the memory of people then living. The liberated peoples had lived under the heel of the oppressor for generations. And fear is even less tolerant than hate.

Statesmen were not free agents at Paris. It was their people who demanded violent punishment and revenge. To secure re-election, Lloyd George had made a campaign on "Hang the Kaiser" and "Pay to the last farthing." Clemenceau had carried a vote of confidence in the French Assembly only upon the fervid assurance that the German race would be dealt with once and for all. Neither of these statesmen could have continued in office on any assurance of moderation. Even in the American people, where suffering had been infinitely less, there was full flow of hate and a determination for violence in punishment.

Herein was the most difficult of all problems which faced that conference and will face the world again. Statesmen at Paris, looking to the future, realized that here were 100,000,000 people in the enemy countries who could not be exterminated and who had to be lived with. If there was to be lasting peace, the people had to be influenced into the paths of peace; they had to be given an alternative more advantageous than war, and, at the same time, they had to have a definite reminder not to do it again. It required a delicate balance of tolerance and grim justice. The liberal-minded wished to discriminate between the "people" in the enemy countries and their leaders, and upon this theory moved toward tolerance.

But fear, hate, and revenge overweighed the scale. By device after device, they appear in the Treaty of Versailles. We shall later recount the consequences.

The Will to Peace[7]

Principally under American and British guidance, the peace conference created the League of Nations. The League was a convenient repository for continuing problems. Of vastly more importance, however, it constituted the greatest experiment and the greatest effort that mankind has ever made to assure the peace of the world. It did not come into operation during the period we are discussing.

Effects of the Peacemaking. We may at this point summarize the effects of the peacemaking upon the seven dynamic forces which make for peace and war.

In the field of ideologies, the hopes for freedom of mankind reached the highest point of ascendancy in all history. Subjection of men and class government seemed on the way out of the world. And as a consequence the foundations of peace seemed far more secure than in all past history.

Destructive economic pressures were vastly increased by the war itself and still further increased by the treaty.

Nationalism in its proper forms of freedom and self-government of peoples made the greatest stride of a century. But within it were seeds of selfishness that were destructive.

Imperialism had not died. There was only a shift of possessions of empire. These shifts left destructive hates and destructive aspirations.

Militarism and aggression were stunned but still alive.

[7]For outline of this force, see p. 20; 140 years prior to World War I, p. 60; in World War I, p. 86.

Fear, hate, and revenge were swept on to new intensities by both the war and the peace.

The will to peace had brought forth the greatest experiment in international maintenance of peace of all history. Mankind was inspired with a new hope.

But underneath it all the old power diplomacy had given scant regard to American ideas about balance of power, military alliances, disarmament, self-determination in border provinces, annexations, imperialism, freedom of the seas, indemnities, economic aims, negotiated peace, the new order, impartial justice, and many others. Altogether, out of President Wilson's twenty-five points, he had fully succeeded in but four or five.

But he had represented the best ideals of America. He made a magnificent fight for them.

CHAPTER VII

The Seven Dynamic Forces in the Twenty Years after Versailles

WE HAVE, in this chapter, to examine the swiftest and most explosive revolution in the whole history of Western civilization.

During this period of twenty years between 1919 and 1939, the seven dynamic forces moved in confusion and in violence. They, with the help of inadequate statesmanship, ultimately thrust the world into a second World War.

They moved with such rapidity and such interaction upon one another that their separate discussion becomes most difficult. However difficult this separation may be, it requires the most critical examination for such lessons as we can perceive. Hindsight is always more assured than foresight. But the hindsight gained from being singed by fire is good training for acquiring foresight. We can perhaps learn something from experience as to how the forces of good are to be made to dominate the forces of evil.

Ideological Forces[1]

The spread of representative government over the whole of Europe up to the Russian border at the time of the Armistice had inspired high hopes of a new era of freedom, peace, and progress for mankind. But soon it was to weaken in a thousand frustrations. The renewed hope of a golden age was transformed into an era of fear plagued by a thousand miseries.

Then came the gigantic revolt from personal liberty and representative government. Man seemed to be fighting blindly for some new way out. He seized upon the word "new" as if it contained salvation in itself, without realizing that the tasks of today were created yesterday.

The age-old idea of enslavement of men to the state returned in two new forms. We have mentioned that Socialism and its brother, Communism, were born even before the first World War. We have mentioned that Fascism had its birth during the war. And it was to find a still more ruthless partner in Nazism. Communism and Fascism were to be rivals, and both were hostile to all liberty.

Indeed, the greatest ideological explosion in all modern civilization was the revolt from the spirit of Liberalism over the world. Beginning with the defeat of the Kerensky regime in Russia in 1917 and the rise of Communism, it broke out again with the rise of Fascism under Mussolini in Italy in 1922, the ascendancy of the military party of Japan in 1931, the rise of Hitler in 1933, and a score of lesser dictators in various parts of the world.

[1]For outline of these forces, see p. 12; before World War I, p. 40; in World War I, p. 82; the Armistice and peacemaking, p. 108.

And the infection of their ideologies was to reach into and modify concepts of liberty everywhere.

The ideologies of Communism and Fascism have much in common. They have in common their political forms of dictatorship, domination by a single political party, brutality, ruthlessness, and rule by terror. They are both determined enemies of free economy and private rights. They are both founded upon sheer materialism. They are both intensely militaristic and imperialistic. They both ruthlessly oppose intellectual and spiritual freedom.

There is one broad distinction between them. Communist revolution is a complete overturn of society in the name of "the proletariat." It is a cult of supposed complete economic equality. Fascism is an overthrow in the name of the elite. It is a cult of national efficiency. There is less murder and "liquidation" under Fascism, but the moral base is no higher. Communism is brutally opposed to all religious freedom. "Religion is the opiate of the people." Fascism seeks to use religion for purposes of the state. There is another distinction in that Communism is a total expropriation of private property to the state, whereas Fascism continues the private ownership of property but compels its operation for the state. Either is slavery. And Fascism came to power largely as the result of middle-class despair over the failures of representative government to repel the inroads of Communism.

These ideologies are of the most militant type. The Communists, in 1917, organized an attack upon personal liberty and representative government over the entire world, with Moscow as their holy of holies and with the gold of Russia to finance it. The Fascists have been somewhat less energetic in foreign penetration, but with no less intent, as witness their Fifth Columns and their Quislings.

Representative government, which seemed to have established itself as a triumphant concept in the world, was left fighting for its life in World War II. Few Americans even today realize the almost total revolt from Liberalism on the Continent, not only in form, but in the beliefs of men. But Americans should observe the march of these revolutions. This gigantic revolt involved 500,000,000 people in Russia, Germany, Italy, Austria, Poland, Estonia, Latvia, Lithuania, Yugoslavia, Turkey, Hungary, Rumania, Bulgaria, Greece, Japan, Spain, and Portugal. And yet the initial overturn from representative government in all but Russia and Spain was accomplished with the loss of but little blood. It is useless to deny that the peoples of many of these countries welcomed this overthrow of freedom. In many of them, the people voted the new ideologies into being.

The soil upon which all these revolutions throve was prepared by the destruction, the miseries, the disillusions and the moral degradation of the war. The peace treaty had responsibilities in its legacies of selfish nationalism and imperialism and in hate, fear, and revenge. The conduct of the dominant powers in the years following the treaty had a responsibility in driving peoples to further desperation.

There were other contributing causes. These were the trumpetings of new Utopias to despairing peoples. And to their propaganda and borings from within, the very freedoms of free government gave full license. Thus freedom was destroyed by the waters from her own well —free speech, free press, and right of assembly.

Racial mores which were yet unacclimated to the freedoms of personal liberty and its self-disciplines led to license. The faulty structure of these new representative governments created a multitude of factions or parties in legislative halls, whereas democracy can really function with stability only in more disciplined party systems.

In the Fascist revolutions, as we have said, the fear of Communism played a considerable part. The Communists bored from within especially by corrupting the labor groups and using them to create disorder. The fear of Communism was the immediate turning point in the movements to Fascism.

Finally, two thirds of the people of Europe, starving and idle, despaired of finding their way out through personal liberty and representative government. Allured by the Fascist promise of food, protection of property, and restored order, they welcomed "men on horseback." They voted most of them into power. Truly, they voted their own doom. And doom of all their freedom it has been.

Initially, these were to be revolutions in the economic systems and political organizations only. But quickly the dictators found that they could not secure economic recovery and political ascendancy without more and more coercion and without suppression of every form of actual or possible opposition. Having lost the whole mainspring of economic production through the loss of confidence and the fears of men, they substituted fear of the concentration camp. Quickly they shifted the ideological pattern into the shapes of despotism, terrorism, and slavery.

Economic Pressures[2]

As we have said above, the economic pressures were a large contribution to the revolt from Liberty. The first

[2]For outline of these pressures, see p. 13; before World War I, p. 44; in World War I, p. 84; the Armistice and peacemaking, p. 113.

World War left the world a hideous economic inheritance. It depleted the best manhood; it destroyed skills; it brought moral degeneration and lifted brutality to a profession. It left damaged or wrecked factories, mines, railways, ships; depleted herds and soil; and ruined orchards. It disrupted the machinery of economic life. It destroyed savings and capital, left gigantic internal and international debts and inflation. The very delicacy of adjustment and international interdependence of the economic life before the war contributed to ruin by the disruption of the machinery of trade and credit. Its net result was to be seen in tens of millions of unemployed, starved, and pestilence-ridden peoples.

To analyze the contribution these disasters made to the revolt from representative government and toward war presents one immediate difficulty. The forces of destruction on the march did not march in step between different countries. They were modified by racial characteristics and leadership. The reactions of political and other pressures affected each country differently. But certain generalizations can be discovered which are of importance to our later conclusions.

After Versailles, all the world except Russia went to work to resuscitate free economic systems. The first task was to reorient economy from purposes of war to civilian production. But they were soon to realize that after total war, it was not a simple process to turn swords into plowshares. Under the absorptions of their economic systems during the war, nations did not feel their real economic wounds until the war was over. All nations were soon to realize that there were wounds in the complicated economic system of industrial age that were deep and festering. These were most severe in the former enemy states and most of the newly liberated nations—with Italy and France but a short distance behind. The United States, Britain and the neutrals suffered less, but even there the shock upon the delicately adjusted economy of the Machine Age was disastrous. And these shocks continued to reverberate over the whole world from the center of worse confusion of the Continent. Britain and America were still strong enough to have pulled out quickly to recovery but for economic shocks and ideological infections from the Continent.

With the Armistice, most nations tried to drop their government-managed or -dictated economics. Most of them first tried to heal the wounds of war the hard way —by freeing enterprise, honoring debts, and stabilizing currencies; stimulating thrift and savings as the basis of recuperation of capital; driving to balance budgets; and generally hoping for the growth of individual initiative, self-discipline, and self-reliance. Practically all governments, in the meantime, directly or indirectly gave support to the unemployed against hunger, cold, and disease. It was the method of healing wounds by the natural growth of cell upon cell, with governmental protection from suffering. The more exhausted countries and those of less vitality on the Continent responded slowly. Other countries, such as Britain, the United States, and the neutrals, progressed on these lines until the more exhausted countries collapsed. In the more exhausted countries, men lost patience with the hard way. And in different countries at different times men's minds began to revert consciously or unconsciously to resurrection of wartime economic regimes as the way out.

As we have said, war organization, even in the democracies, had of necessity to take regimented forms. With the pains of after-war disorganization and the aches of the hard way, men quickly became candidates for public favor who proposed to speed up convalescence by restoring some degree of the coercion economics of war. These ideas were arrayed in new garments of fine colors and heralded as the salvation of mankind. They gave the people hope of a new road out of misery. Everywhere these men promised punishment to economic evildoers, a division of supposed stores of wealth, with assured security and comfort for everybody.

There thus emerged what can perhaps be defined as another ideology—that is what is called "managed economy." Its essential characteristic is an attempt to maintain personal liberty and representative government with some considerable degree of totalitarian methods in the field of economic freedom.

The subject has a relation to the problems of peace and war in many aspects, which we discuss later. It bears upon the revolt from liberty and representative government. From its failure to restore employment came pressure to rearmament as a relief measure. In many countries it was a transition stage in the rise of dictatorships. And it enters into foreign relations through governmental action in foreign trade. It therefore merits some amplification.

Before we discuss the subject further, it is desirable that we define what we mean by economic freedom. To be free, men must choose their callings, bargain for their own services, save and provide for their families and old age. And they must be free to engage in enterprise so long as each does not injure his fellow man. And that requires laws to prevent abuse. And when we use the term "economic freedom," "free enterprise" or "Fifth Freedom," we use it in this sense only, not in the sense of *laissez faire* or capitalistic exploitation. Such freedom does not mean going back to abuses. It in no way inhibits social reforms and social advancement. Economic freedom furnishes the resources for such advancement and flourishes only with such advances.

Laws to prevent men doing economic injury to their fellows were necessary and universal in civilized countries long before the first World War. Government regulation of monopolies, banks, utilities, coinage; prevention of combinations in restraint of trade; government support to credit in times of stress; public works; tariffs; limitations on hours of labor; relief of suffering; etc. might be called "managed economy." The essence is one of degree—that is, the extent of government action and centralization of power. At some point of this expansion of government into the economic field, it begins to stifle initiative and enterprise, with consequences in unemployment and lowered standards of living. At some point it weakens the constitutional safeguard of personal liberty and representative government and begins to trespass upon liberty itself. At these points it could be more appropriately called statism.

The development of managed economy on the continent of Europe covered a varied range of activities and in different degrees of intensity. It included manipulation of currency, credit, and markets. It included huge government expenditures for public works and in other efforts to prime the economic pump, with consequent unbalanced budgets, increasing public debt, and inflation.

Governments sought to lift prices and wages by restriction of production. They undertook the operation of some types of business, and thus included strong draughts of Socialism. They undertook dictation to business, labor, and agriculture, and thus included the strong doses of economic coercion of Fascism. The spirit was hostile to free enterprise. Much-needed reforms of economic abuse were undertaken not through thoughtful development of definite rules of law but by short cuts through wide authorities to bureaucracies. Every advance in economic power of governments brought needs and demands for more and more power.

As these regimes progressed, they overwhelmed legislative bodies with tasks impossible of deliberative digestion. They secured acquiescence of legislators through pressure groups, coercions, and the bait of political privilege. They undermined the independence of legislative bodies. They weakened them by their undermining of constitutional safeguards of liberty. They brought the degradation of privilege. They brought back the very system of ruinous bureaucracies from which the French Revolution had originally started.

Managed economy was thus a mixture of free enterprise, together with Socialism and Fascism. The proportions varied in different countries. We have constantly to remember that free economy is governed by the most delicate of hairsprings—confidence of individual men who operate it; confidence in money, in open markets, in credits, in stability of government finance; and, above all, confidence in the future. And as free enterprise is based upon voluntary co-operative action and security from fear, it was easily stifled by the interferences, uncertainties, confusions, and fear of political action. The way was paved for the full Fascist stage, where production is secured not by confidence of free men but by coercion and fear.

No one country engaged in all of these practices at one time. But Italy, Germany, Spain, and some lesser nations embraced them in part. In France, the attempt by Blum to mix larger doses of totalitarian economics into free economy contributed to the demoralization of the country which had so tended the cradle of economic liberty. It can be observed that every European nation of a totalitarian or managed-economy system turned to the manufacture of arms before they secured employment and war markets.

From the other economic and political repercussions of war aftermaths which we have enumerated, together with the failure of managed economy, the economic collapse on the Continent could not longer be staved off. The crash and panic beginning in Austria in 1930 swept Germany and all Europe, finally dragging the whole world down into the "Great Depression." From the miseries of the depression came renewed impulses which contributed to the revolt from all personal liberty and representative government. One after another, nations comprising hundreds of millions of people went over to dictatorship and Fascism.

Britain and the United States and most neutrals had made real recovery from the war. There were weaknesses. One of the worst in both Britain and the United States, the least-hurt of all nations, was a wild speculative boom. It arose initially from the moderate war inflations, the postwar food and raw material shortage abroad, and the war suppression of housing and other construction at home. The speculative temper was made worse when the Federal Reserve Board and the Bank of England in 1927 yielded to the urgings of Europe to inflate credit further. That action may have staved off the European collapse for a year or so, but inevitable disaster could not be long deferred. The real effect was further to stimulate our own speculative orgy, which finally, in 1929, collapsed, partly of its own weight and partly from foreign causes.

But the real detonator of the crash was central Europe when, in 1931, their panics, their defaults of private and public credits dragged down the entire world. America could have recovered from its own misdoings in a year, but with the European collapse, we were dragged into the depths of depression as great as that which followed ten years after our Civil War. There were many other contributing factors to this depression, but the subject is not part of this discussion.

Managed economy infected Great Britain for a short period only under the Labor Government. That stanch people had shaken it off, and, continuing the hard way, they made real recovery both from the war and the depression. The United States, impatient with recovery from the world depression by the hard way, became infected with managed economy in 1933.

Whether managed economy in the United States had extended over the line where recovery by voluntary and co-operative action of free enterprise was stifled and liberty infringed is not part of this discussion.

There is, however, an illusion and a warning to Americans in all this world experience with managed economy, including our own. The illusion of its advocates is that there can be totalitarian (or coercive) economics and at the same time a survival of the personal liberties of free speech, free press, free assembly, freedom of worship, and free representative government. The moment that managed economy steps over the line where voluntary action, co-operative movement, and individual initiative reign, protest begins. Soon the bureaucracy loses patience with opposition and starts limiting personal expression by direct or indirect coercion. Moreover, when the voters in large numbers become dependent upon the state, the rule of the majority may become tyranny.

This whole period of twenty years was everywhere marked by frantic nationalistic economics. The pressures for individual recovery within nations led to a deluge of increased tariffs, which America followed after some two-score nations had increased their tariffs against us. The many new small nations freed by the war developed such economic and political excesses as to impoverish themselves. Then came special trade agreements; reciprocal agreements; quotas; manipulation of currencies to influence international trade and other barriers to commerce. The whole of these excessive nationalistic economics contributed to world economic disorganization.

The tendency of politicians in each country has been to blame immediate local causes for the world economic collapse, but no capable student of peace and war ignores the fact that the dominant cause was in the inheritances of the war itself. Had there been no war, such a collapse would not have occurred.

Nationalism[3]

Nationalism rose steadily during the whole fateful twenty years. The newborn states expressed it culturally, economically, diplomatically, and in armament, with great vigor. Especially in the economic and military fields did excesses contribute to the general degeneration. Germany

[3]For outline of this force, see p. 13; 140 years prior to World War I, p. 49; in World War I, p. 85; the Armistice and peacemaking, p. 117.

moved under Hitler into the grotesque concepts of racialism and the "Master Race." These concepts were part contribution to their persecution of the Jews and other racial minorities.

In addition to the small countries which set up national existence at the end of the first World War, there were various lands throughout the world which had not progressed so far, but where the ferment of nationalistic agitation was preparing the way to more independence among nations. Such movements were pronounced in China and its resentment of foreign occupation of parts of its territory; in India and Burma for dominion status in the British Empire; and to some extent among the Malayan and other races.

A side issue of explosive character in nationalism of this period lay in the handling of the irredentas of Europe by the Versailles Treaty. There are many of these areas of mixed populations where a reasonable boundary is difficult if not impossible to draw. For any boundaries through the areas of mixed population leave great masses of people separated from their homelands. Nationalistic agitations and repressions began on both sides. With the Treaty of Versailles these boundaries were stretched everywhere to the advantage of the victors. Many festering irredentas still remained, and some new ones were created. The treaty placed many Russians, Lithuanians, and Germans under Poland; it placed many Hungarians, Bulgarians, and Russians under Czechoslovakia, Yugoslavia, and Rumania; it placed many Germans under Czechoslovakia and France, Arabs under Britain, etc. It all added to clamor and chaos.

IMPERIALISM[4]

Imperialism again put its ugly hands into the chaos of these twenty years. Imperialism, punishment, and reparations had shorn Germany of her possessions. When Hitler came to power in 1933, he at once raised the banner of unification of his race and the cry for territory to exploit. His invasions of Austria, Sudetenland, Memel, even before the present war, are evidence enough of the rising imperialism of Germany. Japan took Manchukuo by conquest from China. Italy was aggrieved at her failure to secure imperial possessions at Versailles and undertook the conquest of Ethiopia. The appetite for possessions was not quieted in the world.

And another form of imperialism emerged in this period: that is, the political subjection of nations by penetration of ideologies. By this means the Communists sought to extend the domain of Moscow influence, and the Germans the domain of Berlin influence. By this method Russia at one time gained temporary dominion over Finland, Estonia, Latvia, and Lithuania, and reached into Hungary. She succeeded in Georgia, Azerbaijan, and Outer Mongolia.

Fascism and Nazism have directed their policies to the creation of ideological blocs by such penetration combining them by military and economic alliances. Therefrom we have the "Axis" and its adherents. Nor are these ideological penetrations limited to acquiring territory. They are used to disturb the policies of other countries. Both

[4]For outline of this force, see p. 17; 140 years prior to World War I, p. 51; in World War I, p. 85; the Armistice and peacemaking, p. 119.

Communist and Fascist Fifth Columns worked increasingly to these ends throughout the world in this period.

Militarism[5]

Militarism quickly demonstrated that it was not killed by the treaty. As a matter of fact, its greatest triumph was the defeat of disarmament in the Allied countries.

Communist Russia led rearmament in a stupendous fashion at once after the war. Mussolini immediately built a militarist state as part of Fascism. When Hitler came to power he repudiated the disarmament of Germany and began the building of huge armaments. The military alliances of the Axis which followed provoked vast counter rearmament in the liberal nations.

From 1932 to 1938, the annual arms expenditure of the world increased from about $4,000,000,000 to about $18,000,000,000. Such a sum would have probably relieved most of the acute poverty in the Western World had it been applied to productive purposes. And this sum of $18,000,000,000 compares with $1,500,000,000 five years before the first World War. And it meant a vast military machine in the world whose inclinations turned in 1933 toward war, not peace.

Fear, Hate, and Revenge[6]

We need add little to what we have already said to indicate that the evil forces of fear and its allies, hate and revenge, continued and grew steadily more bitter in

[5]For outline of this force, see p. 15; 140 years prior to World War I, p. 56; during World War I, p. 85; the Armistice and peacemaking, p. 120.

[6]For outline of these forces, see p. 19; before World War I, p. 58; during World War I, p. 86; the Armistice and peacemaking, p. 121.

many parts of Europe from the treaty in 1919 down to 1939.

Wars seldom bring about the brotherhood of man. Hate lives on, and it becomes entrenched in the mores of a people. The defeated are always humiliated, no matter how just the peace. No nation ever recognizes or admits that it was wrong. No leader in that nation would dare to suggest such a thing. We saw Germany, Austria, and Hungary refuse to accept the terms of peace except technically. The forces of new wars began to gather emotional strength the day the treaties of peace were signed.

It is an interesting observation that neither the reactionary Treaty of Westphalia nor the Treaty of Vienna attempted to punish the defeated. Those treaties proved more lasting than Versailles, which, except for its punishments, was far more liberal in character.

And worse still, the process of modern total war, with its hideous brutalities to women, children, and noncombatants, breeds a deeper hate, a greater demand for punishment; and the total humiliations of defeat in modern war create an undying demand for revenge. Certainly this twenty-year period was one of ascending hates. During this time the burden of reparations and international debts left over from the war were unceasing causes of hard feeling. But outstanding in threat to the peace of Europe was the fear and hate between France and Germany. The Hungarians never ceased their hymns of hate against their neighbors for the dismemberment of their territory. The French and Italians, once comrades in arms, steadily developed ill feeling. Hate between the Japanese and Chinese rose steadily from the aggressions of Japan. The Czechs, the Poles, the Baltic states, and the Balkans could not easily forget their centuries of oppression.

However, the British and Americans did allay their hates toward former enemies and gave to them great aid until the rise and threats of the Fascist groups.

Toward America for her generosity and service in saving millions of lives in a score of friendly and enemy nations of Europe, and for her part in the liberation of many of them, came an affection that has never before been witnessed in this world. But aside from this, only in the Western Hemisphere can it be said that universal good will among all the nations made gains in this period.

THE WILL TO PEACE[7]

This twenty-year period represents in the whole history of civilization the greatest definite effort of mankind to organize peace and international co-operation. The League, the World Court, Locarno, Lausanne, the conferences for the reduction and limitation of armaments, the Kellogg-Briand Pact are monuments to that effort.

As the world, twenty years after one dreadful war, blew up in a second and more fearful conflict, all the work of buttressing peace has been condemned as futile. We do not believe that such condemnation is justified. The world will attain peace only by sore trial and error. The League of Nations, above all other efforts, has given us a vast fund of experience. We will elsewhere critically examine the directions of its success and the causes of its failures.

We may emphasize here, however, that it was not the League that brought the collapse of the world into a second total war. The League was the creation of representative government, and when representative govern-

[7]For outline of this force, see p. 20; 140 years prior to World War I, p. 60; in World War I, p. 86; the Armistice and peacemaking, p. 123.

ment and personal liberty died, the League died also. The present war came from the revolt from Liberalism, the rise of totalitarianism, of selfish nationalism, of imperialism, of militarism, of fear, hate, and revenge. These evil forces were not allayed by the Treaty of Versailles. They found roots of growth in it. And the efforts to organize peace failed because of these foul growths.

We cannot avoid the haunting fear that the decline and fall of the League and other liberal efforts were a part of a decline and fall of civilization on the continent of Europe—a vast compound of impersonal forces driving inexorably to some dreadful fate.

The Attitudes of the Principal Nations during the Twenty Years

It is of the first importance that the world examine and understand the experience and lessons from the gigantic peace efforts of the period. But to do so more effectively we will first examine the effect of the six dynamic forces of degeneration upon the attitudes and actions of the principal nations during this time. Especially we must examine the relation of that conduct to the great revolt which precipitated the present war.

This twenty years was a period of heartbreaking divergences of attitudes and degenerations in relations between nations. After the peace treaty Britain, France, Italy, and Japan remained the only substantially armed nations, with Russia rapidly rearming. The British and French, acting together or separately, were able to impose their will upon all Europe up to the borders of Russia. With the Italians, they dominated the League and could determine its European policies. But at once there grew up differences between them, and an entire lack of cohesion in action in their relations with Germany, Russia and the Liberated Nations.

FRANCE AND GERMANY. The dominating factor in French foreign policies was fear of Germany. These fears had dominated French policies for two generations. It is easy to understand French apprehension. As we have said, within the recollection of living Frenchmen, France had been twice invaded by the Germans, her lands and homes destroyed with fire and sword, the best of her manhood killed or maimed. Her population was less than two thirds that of the Germans, and it was not unnatural that she should believe her security could be obtained only by keeping Germany prostrate or by international alliances against her.

In any event, at the end of those four years of the World War, again exhausted and bled white, France was determined to keep Germany in military and economic bondage when she had a chance. Her fears were such that she would not participate in limitations of naval arms except in words, although her naval superiority to Germany was always conceded; she would participate in no reduction of land arms, though armies overwhelmingly greater than those of Germany were always proposed for her defense. She yielded unwillingly to every effort at amelioration of the impossible and unworkable reparations. Meantime, to buttress herself with international support, she was frantically building rings of military alliances around Germany. She drained her resources to arm the Poles, the Czechs, the Yugoslavs, and the Rumanians. She entered into a military alliance with Communist Russia. The reaction of French policies upon the Germans was to heighten every German hatred and to confirm every fear of encirclement and destruction.

France had one of two courses to follow. The one was to hold Germany down by grim force of arms. The other was to join in sustaining a democratic regime in Germany, giving her an economic chance; holding to German disarmament, but joining with other nations to lower all armament and thus relieve economic burdens everywhere. France followed neither course consistently, and the latter least of all. During the whole period from 1918 to 1939, she was the stumbling block to every proposal for world advancement, constantly demanding guarantees for her own security as the price of co-operation with other nations in any direction. At the same time, she alienated her major and natural allies, Italy and Britain.

FRANCE AND ITALY. The French attitude toward Italy drove Italy into the arms of Germany, and thereby greatly increased the menace to French safety. It began when the Italians were denied the promised lands enumerated in the secret treaty upon which they had entered the war. Then followed French affronts and pinpricks. France's repeated rebuffs of Italian advances wasted the period when Italy would have accepted almost any reasonable solution of colonial and naval questions.

Nor was France constant to her major protector, Britain, or to the League of Nations, as witness the abandonment of the British in the economic sanctions against Italy at the time of the aggression against Ethiopia. French conduct generally helped to alienate the United States from all European problems. At this distance, the whole course of French diplomacy, except in certain intervals of Briand's ascendancy, is incredible. We have here the age-old forces of fear and hate doing their suicidal worst.

In the course of this discussion we have frequent occasion to criticize the policy and action of the French Government. We wish to stress the fact that our criticisms are directed at political leaders, not at the nation. It is a tragedy for our civilization that a people of such magnificent virtues and intelligence should have entrusted their destinies, with honorable exceptions such as Briand, to a class of politicians unable to rise to the need of the times. The French people should have every sympathy and support in their blood and tears. We should not lose sight of the fact that it is essential to any real rehabilitation of Europe that France should be restored to a position of weight and influence worthy of her great national qualities.

THE UNITED STATES AND GERMANY. The attitude of the United States of giving aid and support to the building of a representative government in Germany was not confined to the treaty negotiations, but continued in every crisis during the whole life of the Weimar Republic. The friendly offices of Americans brought about the Dawes Commission in 1924, the Young Commission in 1929, the Hoover Moratorium and the Standstill Agreement in 1931, all in endeavors to save the republic from economic collapse under reparations pressure. Our arrangement of the meeting of Premiers at Geneva in 1932 in an endeavor to relax the unnecessary burdens of the treaty, and our calling of a World Economic Conference of 1932 are but part of our interest and effort. In all these efforts we had the full co-operation of Britain and usually of Italy, but always the opposition of the French Ministers.

BRITAIN AND GERMANY. The intermittent and intransigent courses of French policy were a constant anxiety to Britain. Britain did endeavor to support the growth of liberal forces in Germany, but in every crisis had to yield something to France. Outstanding instances of this desire of the British to give the democratic regime in Germany a chance were their opposition to the French occupation of the Ruhr in 1923 and their refusal to join in the French schemes against democratic Germany or the alliance with Russia. British leadership of reconciliation at Locarno gave great hope. Her initiative in the move to admit Germany to the League of Nations, her urging the French to accept the Hoover Moratorium in 1931, her support to the American proposals to strengthen Bruening and German economic stability in 1932 were all instances of British anxiety to strengthen the forces of freedom and economic recovery.

Americans can perhaps better understand British policies in Europe if they will constantly realize that she has always had intermittent spells of isolationism and disgust with continental power politics and continental wars. But finally driven by ascending crises, and without any effective machinery for common action, she falls back upon the familiar methods of balance of power.

Nevertheless, all through the period of German democracy, the British were constantly seeking opportunities to strengthen the liberal forces within Germany. When Germany did revolt from representative government to dictatorship and did become a menace, then Britain supported France and the balance of power against Germany and Italy.

ITALY AND GERMANY. Italian policy has been described as the antithesis of British policy. Whereas Britain seeks to prevent any Power acquiring domination, Italy is on the lookout for rising stars and seeks to throw in her lot with the winning side. She had real grievances from the Treaty of Versailles and from the domineering attitude of France. And indeed, these grievances contributed to the rise and popular support of Mussolini, with his trappings of Fascism and dictatorship. With this ideology, the new Italian Government had initially no sympathy with republican Germany.

GERMANY. Germany came out of the Treaty of Versailles with real and fancied grievances. She deserved punishment. But as we have stated before, that punishment took forms which brought no benefit to the Allies and which made it doubly difficult for the men to succeed who were struggling to liberalize Germany. Certainly, if establishment of representative government is the cornerstone of lasting peace, then many of the Allied acts were most utter folly.

The aggressive and bitterly nationalistic character of the German ruling class has been one of the fundamental causes of European wars for centuries. The almost constant formula of other European nations in repression of Germany has been to divide the race into separate states. But the resultant agitation of this virile people for union has been one of the prime causes of European wars. Even customs union with German Austria was prohibited, and in the subjection of large groups of Germans to Poland and Czechoslovakia was laid a powder train to the new explosion. Added together were the weakening of representative government, economic demoralization, the penetration of Communism, and the growth of real or fancied grievances, which brought Hitler to power.

How just was the German complaint about its treatment is not the whole question. When a nation is humiliated by defeat and becomes indurated with such beliefs and resentments, she becomes hopeless of reasoned action —and this, regardless of real rights and wrongs.

With all these different attitudes, it is not surprising that European developments have been complex and confusing. It would have been surprising if, during this troubled period, the divergent policies in the leading nations had led to solution and peace.

CHAPTER VIII

The Will to Peace during the Twenty Years after Versailles

THE EFFORTS at international organization to preserve peace rose to greater heights in the period of twenty years from 1919 to 1939 than ever before in all the history of man. Great experiments were tried and failed. But from this very experience the world may have found real guidance to the Promised Land. It is our purpose to explore these efforts in this chapter.

THE LEAGUE OF NATIONS

The nursery of the League of Nations was not only set in the middle of conflict among leading nations which we have outlined in the last chapter. It was also surrounded by the grim misery, the strife, the revolution and the ascending nihilism of reaction from the greatest shock that has come to man—total war. An analysis of the League and its results becomes at the same time a recitation of the effect of the seven dynamic pressures and the treatment of the League by the various governments after the war.

The immediate spread of representative government over the world gave a foundation upon which such a liberal institution as the League had a chance to take hold. But, as said above, the League, born of Liberalism, could not survive after representative government had perished.

It is not necessary here to recount the origins of the League of Nations idea. In various forms it had appeared in the discussion of thinking men long before the outbreak of war in 1914. The ideas of military and economic sanctions to be applied collectively by all nations against an aggressor were a part of this thinking. Organizations had been established in various countries to promote the League idea early in the last war—and various drafts had been proposed before the peace conference. But the drafting of the actual League Covenant was done under great pressures for haste and many conflicts of interest. Of necessity, there was much compromise which led to subsequent confusion.

The League Machinery

The League machinery consisted of an Assembly, a Council, a Secretariat, and co-ordinate international organizations. The Assembly comprised representatives of all member nations, meeting once a year and on call for emergencies. In the Assembly, each member state had one vote. The Council, which met periodically or on call in emergencies, envisaged a permanent membership of Britain, France, the United States, Italy, Japan, and certain others elected by the Assembly to temporary membership. The number of these temporary members rose from four at the start to ten, which gave the Council a total membership of fourteen. Action by the Council and Assembly was required to be by unanimous vote with certain exceptions. These exceptions related mostly to procedure, election of members, and exclusion of those members engaged in dispute from the right to vote. In effect, no action of the Assembly could become binding except with the approval of the Council.

With the requirement of unanimous vote of the Council, each of the principal Allied governments of the first World War had in effect a complete veto on any action by the League.

The League membership at one time or another embraced sixty-two nations, constituting about nine tenths of the world's population. The "enemy" countries were to be admitted and were in fact admitted after some years. The United States and a few minor states did not join, while Brazil, Italy, Germany, Japan, and a few others ultimately withdrew, and Russia was expelled.

The permanent Secretariat at Geneva functioned admirably under a secretary-general and an efficient international civil service at Geneva. The International Labor Office was affiliated with the League. The League was entrusted with the duty of establishing and supporting the Court of International Justice at the Hague. And the League encouraged and co-ordinated many other agencies of international co-operation.

The League Purposes

The declared purposes of the League were to establish "international co-operation," achieve "peace and security," "an obligation not to resort to war," "the firm establishment of international law," "maintenance of justice," and "respect for treaty obligations."

The separate fronts of the League's attack upon war were:

1. A commitment of members to respect and "preserve as against external aggression the territorial integrity and existing political independence of all members."
2. A commitment of members to seek settlement of controversies by negotiation, conciliation, arbitration, judicial settlement, and reports upon fact, with a pledge not to resort to war until three months after these processes were exhausted. All these may be called the pacific methods.
3. Agreement that if a member were unwilling to proceed through these alternative processes and went to war, "it shall be deemed to have committed an act of war against all other members of the League." Then all members were committed to consider severance of trade and financial relations and all intercourse with nationals of the offending state. And finally the Council was authorized to recommend economic and military sanctions (Art. 16). All these may be called the force methods.
4. General disarmament was to be vigorously undertaken.
5. There was to be reconsideration of treaties which had become "inapplicable"—peaceful revision.
6. The League was to promote international co-operation in suppression of crime, and advancement of public health, of trade, labor standards, intellectual exchanges, etc., etc.
7. In addition, the League had certain duties and responsibilities in the administration of former German colonies and the former Arab possessions of Turkey.
8. The League was further charged with important duties for the protection of national minorities.

Thus there were five major principles of peace preservation running through the League Covenant. The first one was a joint guarantee against infringement of the *status quo*. The second principle was the commitment to submit all controversies to arbitral procedure or conciliation. The third was to enforce peace by economic and military alliance of members. The fourth was to relieve strain by peaceful revision of onerous treaties. The fifth was to build international solidarity by co-operation in welfare, economic, and intellectual fields.

Thus, the League was to combine in one organization both force and pacific methods of preserving peace. Generally, the principle was called "collective security."

Areas of Success in League Operation

There were two areas of real success by the League:

The first was the settlement of a good many disputes by pacific methods. Several important disputes were brought before the League or its agencies and disposed of in some fashion by pacific methods which prevented bloodshed. Sometimes no tangible final agreement was secured, but conflict was staved off. There were successful solutions in some minor disputes. But even these minor settlements prevented the growth of antagonisms which might have developed into more serious problems. The success in this direction brought prestige to the League. We give a résumé of these actions in the Appendix.

The second area of success was the non-political co-operation between nations and welfare activities. Co-operative action was effective in labor questions; child welfare and refugees; white and black slavery; public health; drug regulation; economic and tariff standards;

double taxation; treatment of nationals; whaling regulations; intellectual co-operation; communications; and various transportation, transit, and power transmission questions. This multitude of services was accomplished partly by way of distributing information, partly by way of international agreements, and is beyond praise. This picture fulfilled every hope of the well-wishers of the League. More, in fact, was accomplished by the League in twenty years in advancement along these lines than in the whole of the previous century.

Areas of Failure in League Operation

The areas of failure are no less instructive. The causes of failure lay in:

1. The survival of power diplomacy.
2. The inability to formulate a European policy of peaceful reconstruction.
3. The total collapse of the force methods in practical application.
4. The failure to secure disarmament.
5. The failure of effort or real intent to revise the onerous treaties and thus make the readjustments between nations which the injustices of the Versailles Treaty, and other treaties marking the end of the war, and normal change constantly required. That failure permitted the growth of an accumulation of conflicts and grievances, with war as the only available solvent.
6. Internal weaknesses in the League structure.

1. Survival of the Old Power Diplomacy. It is important to consider the political climate in which the League functioned.

The League was to be the instrument of co-operation and collective security. It was *ipso facto* to replace and liquidate the old diplomacy, military alliances, balances of power, the Concert of Europe, etc. It was to be the clearinghouse of disputes that might lead to war. But it did not work out this way in practice. The great Powers —Britain, France, Italy, Japan, and subsequently Germany and Russia—and even the smaller Powers, when they became members, preferred to rely upon their own right arms rather than any "common opinion of mankind" or "collective security." The British asserted publicly time and again their resolution to maintain the naval domination of Europe, and the French with equal vigor asserted their determination to maintain the dominant continental land forces. And they jointly resolved to maintain complete military domination of Europe. Various military alliances, such as the Anglo-French Alliance and the Little Entente, were doing business from the start of the League or even before the start. Others grew like weeds all over Europe.

From the League's first day it found itself paralleled by and in competition with the functioning of the old power politics. Before the Covenant was sealed, before the United States had declined to join, power diplomacy was operating with the old vigor. The old order was not dead. The Council of Ambassadors continued to handle matters of common concern after the League began to operate. Not only was the League ignored on many major issues, but many policies for the League were planned outside its halls.

Power diplomacy penetrated the League itself. The hard fact is that nations have friends, and these friendships could be called upon to prevent any action by the

League. And thus the League was pulled and hauled behind the scenes, as in the cases of Hungary, Japan, and Italy. Moreover, nations have friends among officials, institutions, societies, and individuals in foreign countries, and these two were brought into action in creating influence and public opinion in foreign countries to influence League action.

Quickly, also, the important nations established permanent organizations to deal with League affairs, which grew into a sort of periphery of diplomacy around the League. One of their concerns was the possible encroachment of the League upon national sovereignty or upon independence of action by the individual members of the League. A part of the duties of these representatives was to see that no action was taken by the League that would be inimical to their national policies at home. And for this purpose, groups quickly grew up for mutual aid, especially in satellite smaller Powers attached to the major Powers.

Another of the crosscurrents was the urge of the very human egoism in individual representatives for leadership in activities of the League and for prized positions as members of the Council. In these maneuvers, the old power diplomacy clearly showed its hand. One reflex of it was the increase of the number of members of the Council from eight to fourteen.

Out of these same very human qualities the meetings of the League became forums for a vast amount of camp meeting oratory on peace which the world did not take seriously.

The result of it all was materially to lower the prestige of the League.

On the other hand, the Secretariat embraced a group of men and women of great capacity and intelligence.

They believed in the League and served it with most efficient zeal.

2. The Inability of the League to Formulate a European Policy of Peaceful Reconstruction. But more important was the inability of the League to formulate a broad policy for dealing with European problems.

The major scene of danger of war in the world has always been the continent of Europe. Although it was the transcendent need of the times, the League never had a European policy, even at the moment when every European nation was in its membership. The League Covenant, in Article 19, provided not only for revision of treaties which we refer to later on, but there is the implication of consideration to be given to "international conditions whose continuance might endanger the peace of the world." There seems to have been no serious discussion or consideration of the crisis generated by the rise of the Axis. That is, the major danger to the world was ignored by the League.

The League considered that its prime function was to settle controversies. One purpose of the victors in the last war and the real foundation of peace was to implant and hold representative government in Europe. That concept the League never seemed to have grasped and certainly did not vigorously assert or guard.

Fundamentally, the policies of Europe remained in the hands of the larger Powers—with final determination by the old Allies until the general European revolt from Liberalism and the creation of the Axis.

As an indication of the unwillingness of the principal powers to make use of the League to formulate European peace policies, we give in the Appendix a list of nineteen international diplomatic conferences upon important measures in which the League played no part. We give a list of thirty-six military alliances and non-aggression pacts between European states which ignored the League and its potency to keep peace. And we give a further list of twenty violent actions between nations where the League was too weak to intervene or was not allowed to take action.

We do not contend that the League should have been the center of all these conferences or that it should have intervened in all these actions which affected peace and war. But they at least indicate that the League never was able to replace power diplomacy, military alliances, the balance of power, with collective security on its home ground—Europe.

The whole experience would seem to indicate that one of the first functions in the prevention of war is the development of regional policies in the different major areas of Europe, Asia, and the Western Hemisphere.

Most of the broad policies of long-view peace are regional either to Europe, Asia, or the Western Hemisphere. In the Western Hemisphere, the Pan-American conferences had long and successfully performed that function. Certainly the League failed or was unable to formulate a similar broad policy of European co-operation and of constructive peace.

3. THE TOTAL COLLAPSE OF FORCE METHODS IN PRACTICAL APPLICATION. The attempt to use or the failure to use the gigantic powers of force at the disposal of the League against the two first great imperialistic aggressions after Versailles broke the back of the League's authority. The Japanese aggressions in Manchuria in

September 1931, and during the next year at Shanghai, violated every implication of the Covenant in spirit and letter. The authority of the League was here brought to test in dealing with major Powers. The League failed utterly in its dealings with this gross breach of the Covenant, and the real reasons are important to note.

The Council attempted to apply the pacific methods with painstaking persistence. But when these failed, it did not exercise the measures of force. The commercial and political relations of the major Powers in the Council were such, together with the military consequences involved, that they withheld from the League the powers necessary to effective force action.

Following the Council's failure, the controversy was transferred to the Assembly, where the smaller Powers were more largely represented. But despite brave talk about applying the economic sanctions through a world-wide boycott of Japan, they also soon discovered that the major European Powers would not follow. The small Powers were, it is true, insistent on drastic action. But it soon became obvious that they were less intent on remedying the situation in Manchuria than in establishing a precedent of force action which they could later invoke for their own protection in case of aggression by Germany or Russia. Nor could this failure of the League be blamed upon lack of American co-operation, for upon Mr. Hoover's instructions and under the able guidance of Mr. Stimson, the United States consistently supported the League throughout. Finally, the United States injected a new moral sanction—that is, an agreement of non-recognition of territory gained by aggression.

The second defiance of the League came in October 1935, with the flagrant Italian aggression against Ethiopia. In this case, the Council and Assembly voted partial economic sanctions, but Britain would not go the whole distance and France defaulted in even the partial action upon which she had agreed.

Both attempts to apply force were abortive and were terribly destructive to the prestige and effectiveness of the League. It greatly weakened the League's influence even in the field of pacific settlements.

Brought face to face with the application of economic sanctions, it quickly developed that they had deeper implications than appeared upon the surface. The theory was assumed that by use of the economic sanctions or a universal boycott, any nation could be brought to its knees, and that such sanctions were a measure "short of war." That may be true against a weak nation. But it was soon proved that no strong nation would endure such action. Economic sanctions, if effective, involve the internal economic disorganization of the penalized nation, with vast unemployment and the danger of starvation. These are penalties as great as war itself. It soon became evident that strong nations at least will risk war rather than submit to such action.

The advocates of collective military or economic force against evildoers, aggressors, outlaws, or whatever they may be called are also misled by an analogy. That analogy is that every court has a policeman to enforce its decrees. The analogy proved false, in actual experience, for in international cases the policeman is not under the authority of the tribunal and is free to do as he pleases. Stated in another way, there are a score of policemen, each under different command. And it is assumed by theorists that not only the international tribunal but the international community will be unanimous and that there will be no clash of interest among the states not involved in the controversy and who must furnish the policemen.

Moreover, when the question came to practical test, where aggression was so patent as in the invasion of Ethiopia by Italy, or of China by Japan, it was soon proved that those nations can count upon friendly or allied nations, whose interest or whose situations were such that while they might disapprove morally, they could not or would not join in military or economic force. Certainly, the powers of military and economic force, such as the League possessed, proved beyond its strength to exert. When it failed to exert these powers, its prestige was gone. If it exerted them ineffectually, then again its prestige suffered. That is what happened. And in happening, it destroyed the strength of the League in its other field, that of pacific methods.

Later in this book we discuss this dual function of promoting peace by pacific methods and at the same time using force to preserve peace.

4. Failure to Secure Disarmament. Article 8 of the Covenant clearly recognized the need for the reduction and limitation of armaments:

> 1. The members of the League recognize that the maintenance of peace requires the reduction of national armaments to the lowest point consistent with national safety and the enforcement by common action of international obligations.

The United States participated in all League efforts at reduction and limitation of armaments. And the only consequential disarmament was brought about wholly outside the League by the initiative of the United States. The Naval Treaties of 1922 and 1930 brought real reduction and stopped unrestricted naval competition in the world for fifteen years. But throughout, the League, hamstrung by France and the Little Entente, made no contribution.

While lip service was paid to the need for reduction, the subject was shunted from committee to committee for some years, during which, it is true, much valuable technical work was accomplished. Finally, when public opinion on the matter could no longer be ignored, the subject was referred for more exhaustive examination to a "Preparatory Commission for the Disarmament Conference." This body sat intermittently from 1926 to 1931 and produced a fund of valuable material and a most unedifying spectacle in the determination of many governments to avoid coming to grips with the problem. The French were resolved to maintain a vast military dominance of the Continent as a vital major policy. Britain had already reduced her land forces, and while determined to maintain naval dominance over Europe, was always prepared to cooperate with the other naval powers in reduction. The enemy states were disarmed, so far as treaty provisions went, for all time.

Finally, the Disarmament Conference of 1932 was convened, in which, as in previous limitation of armament conferences, the United States took full part. As after some months no serious intent was apparent, the United States delegation, upon the instructions of Mr. Hoover, made a direct and blunt proposal covering the abolition of aggressive weapons and a systematic base for reduction of land armament. These proposals, advanced by Hugh Gibson, chairman of the American delegation, were supported by the technical committees and most of the governments represented. But the French and Japanese opposed the plan. Great Britain submitted an alternative plan which was also buried. It was the last call, not only for disarmament, but for the peace of Europe. President Roosevelt revived and strongly advocated this proposal for reduction of aggressive arms in 1933, but no reply was given him.

The idea was to abolish bombing planes, tanks, mobile guns, poison gas, and submarines; reduce battleships; and reduce armies by a coefficient above the necessary police component. The consequence would be to increase the defensive power of every nation.

Throughout the five years of the Preparatory Commission and the life of the Disarmament Conference, France and her followers effectively blocked all efforts to come to grips with real measures of reduction and limitation of armaments. Only so long as a vast dominant military position could be maintained did the French feel secure. We have referred to this in the previous chapter.

However shortsighted their course, it is far easier to be objective about this sort of thing from our position across the Atlantic. The fact remains, however, that great opportunities were lost.

One of the consequences of this failure was Germany's denunciation of the arms provisions of the treaty. She based her right on the preamble to Part V (Military Clauses) of the Treaty of Versailles:

> In order to render possible the initiation of a general limitation of the armaments of all nations, Germany undertakes strictly to observe the military, naval, and air clauses which follow.

The Germans contended that this was a contract between the victors and vanquished by which the former were to reduce armament. They demanded that this contract be performed. Alternatively, they demanded that they be released from the military clauses. The fact remains that, unless the text was pure humbug, it meant something substantially like the German thesis. It may have been unwise to embody such a phrase in the treaty, but once there, it gave German agitators what they needed most—an appearance of injustice and grievance.

As late as 1932 it would still have been possible to reach an agreement by which Germany accepted the perpetuation of her inferior military status in return for some minor adjustments and face-saving clauses. This would have justified some first measures of reduction on the part of the victor nations—but above all, it would have done away with the dangerous sense of grievance felt by the Germans over the military clauses of the treaty and would have helped Chancellor Bruening to keep alive the German Republic.

It is here perhaps that we find the most tragic failure of the League, or, to put it more accurately, the failure of the member states. For if agreement had been reached on reduction of arms at this time, the effect would have far transcended its importance in terms of figures. It would have removed for a time at least one sense of grievance which led to Germany's revolt from Liberalism, on which Hitler came to power.

5. FAILURE IN PEACEFUL REVISION OF TREATIES. From the League's failure to function in its authority to revise inapplicable treaties came some part of the causes of the present war. Article 19 of the Covenant provided:

> The Assembly may from time to time advise the reconsideration by members of the League of treaties which have become inapplicable and the consideration of international conditions whose continuance might endanger the peace of the world.

It is an exaggeration to say that this article provides for change. All it does is to authorize the Assembly of the League to advise members to reconsider treaty provisions which have become inapplicable and which might constitute a threat to peace. As a matter of fact, even this attenuated reference was based less on recognition of normal evolution in international affairs than on Mr. Wilson's belief that it would afford a method for correcting unwise territorial provisions in the Treaty of Versailles.

This Article 19 was not enough to save the League of Nations. It was disastrous in that it offered no effective means of discussing peaceful change, however necessary it might become. The only alternative that remained at the disposal of governments was the use of force. Here Article 10 stepped in with the provision:

> The members of the League undertake to respect and preserve as against external aggression the territorial integrity and existing political independence of all members of the League. In case of any such aggression or in case of any threat or danger of such aggression, the Council shall advise upon the means by which this obligation shall be fulfilled.

What this boils down to is that, in the absence of any opportunity for change by agreement, any attempt to change the *status quo* must lead inevitably to one of two things—either to war or, on the other hand, to universal tacit acquiescence in aggression and breach of the Covenant. It would be difficult to devise a more effective way of bringing the orderly processes of law into disrepute.

As a matter of fact, Article 19 was no more than the expression of a pious hope that the members of the League would be reasonable. Unless all the members of the Council agreed, there could be no readjustment of provisions that had become irksome or intolerable. That this was inadequate is shown by the fact that although there was frequent appeal for revision under Article 19, it was never put into operation, and for a simple reason. The members of the League who opposed any revision had the power of veto. The Powers who have the better of a bargain will always oppose any attempt at revision.

There can be no doubt that the preponderant judgment of the world was that provisions in the Treaty of Versailles, formulated in the hot emotions of the war, with its violations of President Wilson's Fourteen Points and his "subsequent addresses," were destructive of peace and recuperation in Europe. Mr. Wilson's hope and contention was that, with the cooling of war emotions and a wider vision of reconstruction, these matters would be corrected by the League.

However, the veto power of the Allies over every League action made it merely a tool to preserve "the territorial integrity and political independence" of those Powers and their allies and perhaps worst of all the rickety structure of the jerry-built Balkans—in short, the *status quo*.

Boundary and peace treaties are not inspired documents. Sometimes shifting and unforeseeable conditions render change imperative. Sometimes such conditions are highhandedly and unjustly imposed by treaty on no other ground than that one party is strong enough to compel the other to accept. But relative positions have a way of changing. When the underdog becomes top dog, he is hardly likely to go on considering himself bound by a bad bargain he entered into unwillingly. As a rule, he would be willing to readjust matters without going to war. But if all change is opposed, war is the only alternative to continuing under constraint.

It may be as well to examine specific instances in which peaceful change would have averted violence. One of the clearest recent examples of this is to be found in the handling of the Sudeten problem. Under the terms of the Treaty of Versailles, 3,500,000 German-speaking people were incorporated in the Czech state, which thus did violence to the principle of self-determination on which Czechoslovakia was founded. The protests of these people were ignored, and they were denied a plebiscite. Their annexation to Czechoslovakia was justified at Versailles on strategic and geographical grounds. Perhaps this decision was really imposed by circumstances, but it created a dangerous situation, and, having created it, there was obvious need to keep an eye on it and keep injustice to a minimum.

During many years, this German-speaking minority sought to obtain consideration of their lot, which was made intolerable chiefly by the behavior of petty Czech officials. No doubt their own antagonisms to the Czechs played a part also. They sought to appeal for consideration under the Treaty for the Protection of National Minorities but they got short shrift. Nevertheless, they were convinced that under any reasonable regime they could best work out a solution of their troubles within the framework of the Czech state. Representatives of this minority got no consideration and scant courtesy at Geneva. On appealing to the principal Powers, they were denied a hearing and, in some instances, were given to understand that they were no better than traitors in that they appealed to foreign Powers against their own government. This was a clear case where even a brief inquiry would have sufficed to show the existence of definite grievances and the necessity for some sort of revision if violence was to be averted. And failure to deal with the problem made for the disintegration of all treaties. We discuss this incident further, but in fairness to the Czechoslovak Government it must be said at once that the incorporation of the Sudeten area into Czechoslovakia was the result of French pressure at Versailles and in spite of the expressed misgivings of President Masaryk and Dr. Beneš. They found themselves with a responsibility that should be charged to the great Powers rather than the Czech state.

Another case of insistence on treaty terms regardless of possible consequences is to be found in connection with the military clauses in Part V of the Treaty of Versailles, to which we have already referred in discussing disarmament. It has, however, a wider implication. When the Disarmament Conference met in Geneva in 1932, it was obvious that the German attitude would determine the possibilities of success. Chancellor Bruening took the ground, at once enlightened and practical, that Germany wanted to contribute toward creating a situation where there could be a general reduction of armaments. He did not ask to be relieved of Part V of the Treaty of Versailles, under which Germany was completely disarmed, but suggested some unimportant changes which would have lessened the sense of humiliation and inferiority and would have enabled him to turn the thoughts of Germany away from their sense of grievance to more constructive tasks. The American, British, and Italian governments saw his proposals as opening the way to possible success, but the French Government, clinging to the letter of the bond, declined even to discuss any suggested changes in the treaty, maintaining that the Germans had made a bargain—that they must stick to it.

Chancellor Bruening stated at the time that he felt the greatest contribution that Germany could make to the general cause of disarmament would be to shake off the sense of grievance which might lead to an attempt at forcible revision of the Treaty of Versailles. He was convinced that this was just as much in the interest of Germany as of the other Powers, but saw clearly that if there was to be no relaxation even in the appearance of the military clauses, there was the danger that demagogues could stir up a sense of grievance which would lead to dangerous results. His forebodings were only too well founded. Only a few months after his proposals had been scornfully rejected, Hitler came to power, largely upon the indignation he had been able to arouse in Germany over real and fancied grievances. And liberal government in Germany was destroyed.

Here we have another example of the inadequacy of concessions made too late. As soon as Hitler came to power, the French Government manifested a quite different attitude and made a series of proposals which would have been more than adequate while Bruening was in power. Greater and greater concessions were offered by France and rejected by Hitler. And even in France there was a considerable feeling that if Chancellor Bruening had been met in a reasonable way, and helped to dispel the sense of wrong and humiliation, it is highly improbable that Hitler would have succeeded in gaining mastery of the government. The failure to act reasonably on this matter contributed to the success of the Nazi party, with all its disastrous consequences.

Bearing upon this question of revision of treaties, the

League had certain duties in protection of national minorities. But the intervention of the League was greatly limited and the task delicate. The very existence of this authority no doubt had a beneficent influence. A number of solutions were found and actions taken in such cases. But the real cancers of Europe—the irredentas—were untouched. That would have involved revision of treaties and boundaries. This malady of irredentas became one of the contributing causes of the second World War.

We believe it is desirable further to emphasize this whole question. One of the greatest and most disastrous of all defects in methods to promote peace, which was proved by League experience, was on the question of revision of treaties.

The pacific methods of preserving peace by conciliation, arbitration, or judicial settlements are based upon existing treaties, and they become instruments to maintain those treaties, no matter how unjust. Experience now demonstrates that there are whole areas of most dangerous controversies which rise from the pressures of change in the relations of nations. Such are the cases we have mentioned of treaty provisions imposed after the heat of war, shifts in economic pressures, and population pressures. There are also the backward nations which become conscious and capable of self-government, governments which fail in their obligations to minorities, boundaries which become inappropriate, and a score of other questions. In the main, arbitral questions are those of damages, boundary disputes, and the rights of citizens based on existing documents. Unless the possibility of revision of treaties can be brought into active reality, then neither can real aggression be defined nor can pacific processes function.

It will be objected that a defeated Power must observe a treaty concluded at the end of a war. We may as well recognize that the length of time during which the defeated Power will continue to observe the treaty will be largely dependent on (a) how harsh the treaty may be upon the defeated people as a whole, and (b) the time it takes the defeated Power to regain strength. If the treaty is unduly harsh, it will be observed just so long as the defeated Power remains too weak to disregard it with impunity. But it is not realistic to expect a defeated Power to go on accepting an intolerable position when able to throw off the bonds of the treaty. We would do well to base our thinking on the recognition that treaties are on no superhuman plane; that they are sacred only as commercial contracts are sacred. Treaties forced upon nations are not upon the same plane as those that are entered into freely and willingly.

All these analogies were indulged in after the last war whenever there was an appeal for revision. The opposition was on high moral grounds. The world was flooded with speeches on the "sanctity of treaties," and it was represented that any attempt to reconsider a single article of the Versailles Treaty was nothing less than a sinister attempt to undermine its entire fabric and must be resisted as such by all law-loving people. This propaganda was so successful that many people were led to believe implicitly that all change was to be resisted on high moral grounds. We can agree as to the sanctity of the pledged word—but most of this talk meant something quite different. What was really meant was not the "sanctity" of treaties but the "immutability" of treaties or the "sanctity of the *status quo*."

Each and every plan for preserving peace, whether

it be the Pax Romana, the balance of power, the legitimist theory at the Congress of Vienna, or collective security at Versailles, however divergent they may appear outwardly, have one thing in common. They set up a new order, and knowing it to be good, they provide that it shall be kept unchanged. On the surface this may appear logical and prudent—but it is a vital defect. For change, instead of being the enemy of peace, is essential to its preservation.

If we are going to accomplish anything in our time, we must approach our problem in the knowledge that there is nothing rigid or immutable in human affairs. History is a story of growth, decay, and change. If no provision, no allowance is made for change by peaceful means, it will come anyway—and with violence.

6. Internal Weaknesses in the League Structure. One of the weaknesses of this great experiment was inherent in the Covenant itself. Its articles left several gaps and conflicting interpretations. This led to endless legalistic discussions of constitutional construction. Where controversies were brought before the League, the parties resorted to every artifice to avoid League jurisdiction. Whole volumes have been written upon these questions, with interminable discussions of the interpretation of words and phrases of the Covenant and the use of hairsplitting distinctions and disputes to contest its authority or to avoid action. The Covenant's gaps were never cleared up, although various attempts were made to do so.

An indication of such confusion is to be found in the provisions governing the commitments of members. It starts with the positive agreement in Article 12 that "the members of the League agree that should there arise among them any dispute likely to lead to rupture they *will* submit the matter either to *arbitration* or *judicial settlement* or to *inquiry by the Council* and they agree in *no case* to resort to war until three months after the award. . . ."

These commitments became less positive in Article 13: "The members of the League agree that whenever any dispute shall arise between them *which they recognize to be suitable* for submission to arbitration or judicial settlement and which cannot be satisfactorily settled by diplomacy they will submit the whole subject matter to arbitration or judicial settlement."

The commitment becomes still less positive in Article 15: "If there should arise between Members of the League any dispute likely to lead to a rupture which is *not* submitted to arbitration or judicial settlement in accordance with Article 13, the Members of the League agree that they will submit such matter to the Council. . . . The Council shall endeavor to effect a settlement of the dispute . . . and [under varying circumstances] the Council may make public a statement of the facts and of its conclusions regarding the same."

Whether members were completely committed *to submit* questions went to the very heart of the League. Despite interpretations which might be put on the Covenant it developed that nations would not pledge themselves in advance and in unknown contingencies and unknown claims to arbitral or judicial verdict by some tribunal, the personnel and constitution of which could not be foreseen. Perhaps the original intent of the framers of the League was complete commitment to this, but they were not able to get it wholly accepted in the

Covenant. The subsequent British attitude that they could not be bound to submit any dispute to be decided by an international body of uncertain character and composition was probably the general attitude of members who expressed it less frankly. That attitude would seem to have torn the heart out of the pacific sanctions of the League.

In any event, the constant conflict of views over jurisdictional and interpretative questions weakened the League and some nations even withdrew over such disagreements. The experience of the League seems to prove that the Covenant, as framed, attempted too detailed and too binding and at the same time too indefinite an agreement for practical working in respect to pacific methods. Had the whole of the articles on methods of pacific settlement of controversies been condensed into a simple declaration of purpose and a general direction to the League to promote peace, it would have probably proved more binding and in practice less disintegrating to the League setup.

Another primary difficulty was that the League was founded upon two entirely different concepts, one organizing the preservation of peace by military or economic force, and the other the prevention of war by settlement of controversy through pacific methods. The League undertook to carry out its mission by combining both methods. The two concepts proved to be in both philosophic and practical conflict. The idea of promoting co-operation by threatening war weakened the influence of the League in persuasion to pacific methods. Nations were not willing to accept jurisdiction of the League when the end might be such penalties.

The question of the borderline where pacific methods

were to be abandoned and force introduced raised another weakness. The original assumption was that this borderline could be so clearly defined that anyone was an aggressor who refused to settle controversies by pacific methods, or further that aggression was always proved by military invasion. The economic and military force was to be then applied. Sometimes, in flagrant cases, aggression could be so defined.

But aggression does not necessarily begin with actual or threatened military invasion. Nations may be in subjection as the result of aggression long previous. Such nations have a right to be free from oppression even if it takes war. It may not be aggression to aid them to freedom by military means. And aggressions may comprise economic domination or pressure such as boycotts from other nations until they become intolerable and military action is justified in defense. It may be in provocative action or even in provocative words, which humiliate nations or reflect upon their honor.

Another difficulty of defining aggression is that treaties represent the *status quo* of nations at a given moment. Many controversies and current incidents which need to be quieted are based upon insistence on maintaining such an established relationship. Pacific methods are indeed applicable to a large number of run-of-the-mine international difficulties. But those which arise from treaties which were onerous to start with or have been made inapplicable by a thousand circumstances raise problems which are beyond arbitration and judicial decisions.

For arbitration or judicial settlement is necessarily based upon existing treaties. Such action is inherently an assumption of maintaining the *status quo* of such treaties. Thus, these processes are not usually applicable to fundamental changes in treaties. In any event, after long debate by the League in trying to define aggression as refusal to accept pacific methods for the settlement of controversies or to entrust to the Council full authority to make such a determination, the idea failed of acceptance by a large majority of its members. The net of all this seems at least to affirm that the Covenant attempted too detailed a program.

The Effect of American Non-Participation

The American opposition to joining the League was in some part due to sheer vindictive hate against President Wilson. At one period in the Senate debate, however, a less rigid attitude on Mr. Wilson's part would have secured ratification with reservations which were, in fact, immaterial to the larger purposes of some form of organized international co-operation. This opposition could not have prevailed, however, if there had not existed a debatable ground which troubled many Americans. It came largely from the feeling that other features of the Treaty of Versailles were far from the ideals for which America had joined the war. The specific argument in the United States against joining the League, however, revolved around the supposed commitments to a military alliance and abrogation of sovereignty. Such questions presented no difficulties to the European Powers, as they understood perfectly that their veto power as members of the Council and the pressures they could bring to bear would prevent any such interpretations. The obvious ganging up on the United States during the treaty negotiations was the ready answer to American argument for this sort of protection to the United States.

The question of what the destiny of the League would have been had the United States joined is purely speculative. Certainly, Europe and many Americans blamed its failure upon our absence. This constant condemnation of the United States was itself a confession of inability of Europe to keep the peace. At one moment the League embraced every country in Europe and seemingly could have settled upon a European policy of peace.

At the first real threat to world peace from outside Europe (the Japanese-Chinese conflict), the United States co-operated fully with the League, yet that worst of League failures was made because of lack of cohesion among the great Powers of Europe. Likewise, the United States participated in the disarmament and many other international conferences with a full will to succeed.

In considering the possible effect of American participation in the League it must be remembered that the old power diplomacy would in any event have dominated Europe because of the fundamental determination of Britain and France to maintain military domination and to settle the important European policies outside the League.

Thus, the assumption that the United States could by membership in the League have prevented a second World War is a very large assumption that the United States would have been willing to resist the military power of France and England in order to carry out her original ideals of peace. Moreover, it is an assumption that all the other destructive forces set in motion by the treaty and nations acting outside the League could be controlled by the United States.

In any event, time proved that there was no moment after the defeat of adherence to the League Covenant in the Senate when any political party could carry the League with the American people. And no political party did thereafter propose it. The constant refrain in the news columns of conflict, military alliances, intrigue and power politics from Europe was a requiem on American participation. The fact that every President since the war —Harding, Coolidge, Hoover, and Roosevelt—failed by every influence to secure approval of the Senate even to membership in the World Court is evidence of the hardening of American reaction. And this is written regretfully by the authors of this book, who ardently supported adherence to the League and the Court as at least an experiment in preserving peace.

CHAPTER IX

Peace Organization outside the League from 1919 to 1939

DURING THE twenty-year period between the first and second World Wars, the will to peace was manifested in many activities conceived and carried on outside the League. In the Appendix we list nineteen such cases, and the list is by no means exclusive. We here discuss those of greatest importance.

INTERNATIONAL LABOR OFFICE (1919)

The International Labor Office was created by Part 13 of the Versailles Treaty. In the preamble to this part of the treaty, it is stated that "a peace can be established only if it is based upon social justice . . . conditions of labor exist involving such injustice, hardship, and privation to large numbers of people as to produce unrest so great that the peace and harmony of the world are imperiled."

The International Labor Office has proved a most beneficent institution. Although it has little relation to the direct problem of peacemaking, it has an indirect value as a constant stimulant to international co-operation.

WASHINGTON CONFERENCE OF 1921–22

The Washington Conference in 1921–22, called by the United States, was not wholly devoted to naval reduction and limitation. It sought, by treaties, to improve the whole climate of peace in the Pacific area.

In November 1921, the delegates of France, Great Britain, Italy, Japan, and the United States, under the outstanding leadership of Secretary Hughes, reached an agreement on the limitation of ships over 10,000 tons. No agreement could be reached upon cruisers, destroyers, submarines, and auxiliary ships. In capital ships, building programs were abandoned, and some partially completed ships were scrapped.

The principle established was a ratio of naval strength responsive to naval needs and strategic equality. As between the three strongest naval Powers, the United States, Great Britain, and Japan, the ratio was established at 5-5-3, and 1.75 each to France and Italy in ships over 10,000 tons and with guns above 8-inch caliber. The treaty fixed the maximum tonnage of all the larger types, capital ships, aircraft carriers, and cruisers. In order to induce Japan to accept the ratio, the United States undertook not to fortify the Philippines and Guam. Great Britain gave a similar undertaking as regards Hong Kong and various other Pacific possessions.

Japan was already committed by the mandates agreement of the Versailles Treaty not to fortify a number of islands specified by name "and any insular territories or possessions in the Pacific Ocean which Japan may hereafter acquire." But she promptly did fortify them without awaiting the approval of the League.

One of the greatest of all accomplishments of Secretary Hughes was the comprehensive way in which he led the conference in dealing with Pacific and Far Eastern questions, in which the representatives of China, Belgium, Holland, and Portugal participated. Two major treaties, outside the Limitation of Arms Agreement, were agreed upon.

By the Four Power Treaty the United States, Great Britain, France, and Japan guaranteed each other's insular possessions in the Pacific and provided for peaceful solution of controversies about them. The chief significance of this treaty was the provision that on its ratification the Anglo-Japanese Alliance should terminate.

The Nine Power Treaty guaranteed respect for the territorial integrity of China and the "Open Door." It provided "that, whenever a situation arises which in the opinion of any one of them involves the application of the stipulations of the present treaty, and renders desirable discussion of such application, there shall be full and frank communication between the contracting Powers concerned."

The great purpose of these treaties was to give China an unmolested chance to recover from the anarchy of revolution in which she was then plunged. She was unable, however, in the following ten years to build up the national solidarity necessary to defend herself adequately.

London Naval Conference of 1930

We may here digress from chronology to show the continued American effort in naval reduction. In 1927,

President Coolidge issued invitations to a naval conference at Geneva to deal with cruiser, destroyer, submarine and other craft upon which the Washington Conference had failed to find agreement. This conference failed also.

As these craft constituted two thirds of naval strength, and great competitive building was going on, Mr. Hoover, in March 1929, through Mr. Gibson, who was then at the preparatory Arms Conference at Geneva as the American representative, proposed another conference to deal with the subject. It was finally settled that the conference should be called in London. The President, through the able and patient negotiation of Secretary Stimson, Ambassador Dawes, and others, took the precaution of settling the main lines of agreement in advance by direct negotiations with the various Powers.

The conference came to agreement and placed further effective reductions upon all craft, including battleships. This agreement held until it expired in 1936, when the Japanese refused to renew it.

This treaty fully established the parity of the American Navy with that of the greatest other Power, and by this American leadership, billions of dollars of waste in competitive building were saved and much international ill will was avoided.

The Permanent Court of International Justice (1922)

The idea of establishment of a world court which could decide questions between nations suitable for justiciable determination, as distinguished from subjects for conciliation and arbitration, had long been advocated as having a part in the creation of lasting peace. The idea was developed particularly at the Hague Conference of 1907. The Covenant of the League of Nations provided for the adoption of a plan for the establishment of such a Permanent Court of International Justice. "The Court shall be competent to hear and determine any dispute of an international character which the parties thereto submit to it. The Court may also give an advisory opinion upon any dispute or question referred to it by the Council or by the Assembly."

The Statute of the Court was worked out by the League with the aid of the ablest jurists in the world in consultation with the foreign departments of the principal governments; in this, Secretary Bainbridge Colby ably participated.

The Protocol covering agreement to the Statute was completed late in 1920 and submitted to the various nations for adherence. The members of the League signified their adherence, and the Court opened February 15, 1922.

President Harding and Secretary Hughes recommended the Protocol to the Senate in 1923, despite the fact that the United States was not a member of the League, with recommendations as to special agreement by which the United States would participate in all questions respecting the Court. The Senate approved it three years later, but with reservations concerning Advisory Opinions that would require serious alteration in the Statute of the Court. No modification of the attitude of the Senate could be obtained, despite the urgings of President Coolidge and Secretary Kellogg. In 1929, Mr. Hoover asked Mr. Elihu Root to go to Europe and endeavor to find a formula meeting the Senate reservations. This Mr. Root was able to do, and Mr. Hoover and

Secretary Stimson repeatedly urged it upon the Senate, but without avail. President Roosevelt and Secretary Hull have likewise urged it, but unsuccessfully.

The Court has functioned under eminent judges and has successfully resolved some seventy international controversies. The Court, however, received a blow, especially in American opinion, when in 1931 it gave a decision on a case affecting a customs union between Germany and Austria in which the judges voted 7 to 8, largely, it is alleged, on purely nationalistic grounds.

The Court can serve a most useful purpose in preserving peace in a sane world, and such incidents as this could be solved by disqualifying any judge of the nationality of one of the parties to the case from sitting in judgment.

Locarno Treaties (1925)

The Locarno Agreements of October 16, 1925, marked a real attempt to heal the wounds of war and to allay the ancient Franco-German feud. Various attempts to bring about better relations during the previous three years finally found a propitious moment when Austen Chamberlain, Briand, and Stresemann, all men of good will, were at the same time Foreign Ministers of Britain, France, and Germany respectively. A series of treaties resulted in mutual guarantees of the frontiers of France, Belgium, and Germany, with a supplementary guarantee by Great Britain and Italy; arbitration treaties between Germany, on the one side, Belgium and France, on the other; treaties of mutual assistance between France, Poland, and Czechoslovakia in case of aggression. The agreements also provided for the admission of Germany to the League of Nations.

This Locarno settlement represented a brave attempt at regional agreements to solve particular problems. The spirit of these settlements was more important than the actual achievement. At the ceremony of signature in London the oratory became lyrical. Chamberlain described the pact as "the real dividing line between the years of war and the years of peace." Briand said that "in the light of these treaties we are Europeans only." And finally Stresemann, not to be outdone, appealed: "Let each one of us first be a citizen of Europe linked together by the great conception of civilization which imbues our continent."

Some things may, however, be observed about this settlement. Except for lip service, it totally ignored the League, whose real function it was to provide a policy of reconciliation in Europe. Beneficent as it was, it did represent the human quality of Ministers of Foreign Affairs to want the stage. Its spiritual forebear was essentially the Concert of Europe, not the League. And behind it was still the destructive drive of six of the seven dynamic forces which it had done little to remedy or to allay.

The end of the Locarno Agreement was indeed sad. Hitler, alleging that the Franco-Russian Military Alliance had violated the Locarno Agreement, sent his troops into the Rhineland (March 7, 1936) on the ground that Germany was released from her Locarno obligations.

There is no doubt that, under any reasonable construction, this step called for action under the Locarno Agreement. But in the meantime, great fissures had grown up between Britain, France, and Italy. France appealed to Britain and Italy for military assistance. France and Belgium would not act alone—partly because they felt need of support—possibly through fear of alienating Great Britain. Italy was fully engaged in her Ethiopian campaign and, smarting under economic sanctions from Britain and France, was hardly disposed to take military action against Germany on behalf of France. The British Foreign Office found difficulty in seeing any "flagrant violation" or any "unprovoked act of aggression." It was considered that Germany was merely sending her troops into German territory and that this hardly called for steps that might end in war. In these few short years a situation had developed where not one of the guarantors would act to save the Locarno system from ignominious collapse. Neither did the League intervene.

The Kellogg-Briand Pact (1928)

On June 20, 1927, Mr. Briand, then French Minister for Foreign Affairs, proposed to the American Government a bilateral treaty renouncing war between the United States and France. Secretary Kellogg replied to this proposal on December 28 with the suggestion that, instead of a bilateral declaration, an effort be made to secure general acceptance of the project.

As a result, the Kellogg-Briand Pact was signed in Paris on August 27, 1928, with reservations by some Powers to make war in self-defense, although, of course, Mr. Kellogg maintained that the right of self-defense was inherent in the pact itself.

This pact which was originally signed by fifteen governments, including all the principal nations, has considerable significance in the moral definition of war and the implementing of public opinion for the preservation of peace.

The idea had been advanced over a generation and is fundamentally to outlaw war morally, just as society outlaws crime. The advocates of the "Outlawry of War" insisted that the attempt to control and humanize methods of warfare merely tends to recognize war itself as inevitable and almost respectable; that the evil itself will not be extirpated so long as war has a recognized place in the field of international relations.

They held that international agreement on this principle would at least establish standards of conduct. The question, of course, at once arose as to enforcement, any form of which would trespass upon the functions of the League and possibly other existing peace machinery. The common view was, however, that at least at the start it must depend for enforcement upon moral force, enlightened public opinion, and the fidelity of nations to agreement. The essential part of this treaty was embodied in two articles, as follows:

ARTICLE I

The High Contracting Parties solemnly declare in the names of their respective peoples that they condemn recourse to war for the solution of international controversies, and renounce it as an instrument of national policy in their relations with one another.

ARTICLE II

The High Contracting Parties agree that the settlement or solution of all disputes or conflicts of whatever nature or of whatever origin they may be, which may arise among them, shall never be sought except by pacific means.

The moral vitality of the pact was somewhat reduced by its reservations, but it was strengthened by the action of the United States under the leadership of Mr. Hoover and Secretary Stimson during the Japanese-Chinese conflict of 1932. It was then proposed that territorial or other gains made in violation of the pact should not be recognized by other governments. Such a non-recognition declaration was signed by nearly all nations of the world in respect to that act of aggression.

It is a significant fact that no important representative government has ever violated the pact. Totalitarian Germany, Russia, Japan, and Italy have all done so.

Briand's United States of Europe

M. Briand's proposals, undertaken under authority of the League, for a "United States of Europe" have caused a great deal of confusion in discussions as to the possibilities of international federation and the building of supergovernments. Most people have not gone beyond the title, and this title is entirely misleading. It is generally assumed that what M. Briand had in mind was to amalgamate the many nations of Europe under a single central government. This illusion has served to convince many people that a drastic plan of welding together all the nations of Europe must be practical because it was advocated by a practical statesman and was seriously discussed by the governments of Europe.

Briand proposed no more than an organization to serve as an adjunct to the League of Nations to facilitate the solution of problems regional to Europe. Its intellectual progenitor was the Concert of Europe rather than the United States of America. In fact Briand was preparing a definitely organized Concert of Europe. He said, in putting it forward to the Assembly of the League:

> It cannot be a question of a real United States, because each nation of Europe must retain its sovereignty. But since Europe is geographically a unit, there are problems which exist for all. The

economic question should be the first one to be considered, but even in political and social problems, it would often be to the advantage of the various countries to meet and solve questions in common. . . .

Briand was most specific in his statements that the proposed organization was not in any way to affect the absolute sovereignty of its members and their complete political independence. In spite of this, much of the current discussion is based on the assumption that he proposed a "federation" of Europe—that is to say, a central federal government. Study of the correspondence fails to reveal any ground whatever for this assumption. On the contrary, Briand is at pains throughout to make it clear that what he has in mind is to promote "study, discussion, and adjustment of problems which might be of common interest." He proposes "determination of the field of European co-operation—general economy, economic machinery, communications and traffic, finance, labor, hygiene, intellectual co-operation, interparliamentary reports, etc."

All this was clearly a plan for co-operation limited to the European field rather than for federal government—a sort of subsidiary League of European Nations. The plan was viewed with a good deal of skepticism by the League, but Briand was authorized to sound out the various twenty-seven governments, twenty-six of which replied. All of them made reservations of one sort or another. Some felt disarmament must come first; some feared it would weaken the League. Some raised questions of the equality of nations; there was question as to the possible admission of Russia in dealing with questions of free economic systems. The project got nowhere. A Commission of Inquiry for European Union was set up to study the problem. It met three or four times without making any progress, and soon lapsed into a comatose condition. The men who might have given it an impulse were gone. Stresemann had died. Chamberlain was no longer in office, and Briand no longer enjoyed the same free hand under the governments of Tardieu and Laval. The fact that Briand did not envisage or advocate setting up the United States of Europe in the sense that it has been generally understood does not mean that there was no importance in his proposal. As a matter of fact, the regional proposal is probably of greater value because time may prove that this was the first important step towards systematic regional treatment of world problems—a method which would seem to be dictated by common sense and to offer real hopes of progress and achievement.

During this period, the United States made other efforts to combat the vicious forces which were undermining peace and stability in the world. The Economic Conference instigated by Mr. Hoover's administration in 1932 for removal of trade barriers and the stabilization of currency met at London in 1933, but did not meet the approval of Mr. Roosevelt. As we have said elsewhere, at the first Japanese aggression on China in 1931, the United States co-operated with the League in attempts to protect China. When the second Japanese aggression on China occurred in 1937, President Roosevelt secured the calling of a conference of the signatories of the Nine Power Treaty, but it was unable to accomplish anything. When the Munich crisis arose in 1938, Mr. Roosevelt and Secretary Hull exerted the "good offices" of the United States in urging settlement. And President Roosevelt repeatedly proposed undertakings toward peace to the Axis governments. Of more successful issue, however, was the strengthening of Pan-American co-operation under the unflagging leadership of Secretary Hull and Under Secretary Welles.

Other Peace Efforts in Europe—1919–39

We have given in the Appendix a list of many other peace efforts outside the League. It is certain that hundreds of statesmen and millions of citizens worked to this end. The numerous conferences and the sweat of good men are proof that the will to peace was struggling for a chance.

Perhaps even military alliances can be interpreted as efforts to keep the peace—or balance of power. Non-aggression pacts certainly have more of a peace flavor.

But the whole failure of them presents a disheartening picture—attempts of old diplomacy to put temporary lids upon growing explosive forces underneath and, above all, a failure to realize prior to Hitler that the one hope lay in sustaining representative government in the former enemy areas.

And never to be forgotten was the undermining of the whole will to peace by the flagrant repudiation of non-aggression and other treaties which had been entered into in full free will by Hitler, Mussolini, and Japan. No one can say that Locarno, the Kellogg Pact, the Four Power and the Nine Power treaties were dictated or forced upon them.

Summary of the Forces Leading to the World Explosion of 1939

In the last two chapters we have outlined the movement of the seven dynamic forces in the twenty years after Versailles. It requires but a few words to indicate their cumulative effect in the explosion of the World War of 1939.

Again, as in 1914, the immediate causes of the gigantic explosion into the present war were only superficially to be found in the immediate incidents. Again the real causes lay in the dynamic forces of ideologies, economic pressures, nationalism, imperialism, militarism, and the complexes of fear, hate, and revenge.

It is not clear at what point in matter of time the face of the world began to turn from peace toward war. Certainly, at the end of 1933, confidence of economic recovery from the last war and continued peace was general in men's minds, and nowhere was such an immense catastrophe as another World War thought possible. It is equally certain that four years later, during 1937, men everywhere had become fearful, and all the world had joined in arming against renewed war.

It might be remarked that prior to the outbreak in 1914 this change in men's minds took place scarcely thirty days before that outbreak. The change at the present crisis was at least two years before the explosion, the delay of which might be attributed to greater reluctance at starting war or to more capable effort to maintain peace. The observation is a slender tribute to world progress.

The political turning point was probably the refusal of France in 1932 to co-operate in support of representative government in Germany, with the consequent overthrow of the republic by Hitler, with its sequence of Fascist revolutions in some fifteen nations.

Beginning in 1934, ideologic forces rose steadily to a full and fierce world-wide conflict. Fascism and Communism were at war with each other in every respect except actual gunfire. Russia on one side, Germany and Italy on the other, were planting Fifth Columns and propaganda, endeavoring to create internal revolutions in each other's territory, and both executing each other's sympathizers and agents. The Anti-Comintern Pact by Germany, Japan, and Italy was signed late in 1936. Russia, Germany, and Italy had a hand in creating the Spanish Revolution beginning in 1936. The mortal conflict between these ideologies was the more evident when the Fascist Powers gave military aid to Franco in Spain while Communist Russia and the French Government gave like aid to the Republican Government.

Both the Communists and Fascists also carried on war against the democratic governments everywhere with Fifth Columns and propaganda. In the American recognition agreement with Russia in 1933, that country agreed not to stimulate such propaganda but promptly violated the agreement by subsidizing subversive action in the United States. Thus ideologic forces were explosive enough.

Economic pressures induced by the depression had begun to relax with the turn to recovery in the spring of 1932. But many forces, economic and political, intervened to retard recovery, and the world as a whole by 1939 had found little relief from unemployment and a distracted agriculture. The World Economic Conference in 1933 had failed to give relief from unstable currencies and mounting trade barriers. How far these pressures turned nations to making arms and armies as a method of relief cannot be surmised.

Nationalism ran riot in economics by increased trade barriers, through new devices of special and exclusive agreements, quotas, manipulated currencies, and restrictions on production. And in the Fascist countries, nationalism took on forms of extreme racialism, with persecution of minorities and the Jews.

The old monster of imperialism revived in Japan's conquest of Manchuria in 1931, Italy's conquest of Ethiopia in 1935–36, Japan's revived conquest of China in 1937, and the whole purpose of the Axis in the same year.

Militarism did not die even in the victorious countries, and was fed by the French alliances before the Fascist rise. It was obviously an integral part of the whole totalitarian philosophy and organization. After the failure of the Disarmament Conference of 1932, the military expenditures of the world rose from about $4,000,000,000 per annum to about $18,000,000,000 in 1938.

Hate, fear, and revenge were rampant, not alone from nationalist inheritances of the last war, but from the added fuel of ideological conflict.

In these last years before the war, the will to peace still strove to find a way out. It was sustained, partly by the memory of the horrors of the last war, partly by the efforts of statesmen of good will, particularly in Britain and in the Western Hemisphere; but the destructive forces in Europe and Asia, cultivated by malign leadership, had reached the explosion point. Yet the peoples themselves in no country wanted war. When it came in Europe in 1939, and America in 1941, it came with no popular enthusiasm in any nation. Unlike 1914, there were no bands, no flowers, no flag waving, no cheers.

PART III

CHAPTER X

The Foundations of Lasting Peace

SOME DEDUCTIONS FROM EXPERIENCE

EVEN WITH VICTORY, after the dreadful degenerations of these thirty years of war, revolution, and disorder, if Western civilization is to be saved from another relapse into the Dark Ages, it must be saved at the peace table. Never will humanity need more objectivity, more tolerance and more vision, more open and more prayerful minds.

Again we may repeat, we are not here proposing a plan for peace. We are discussing, from an analysis of experience, the principles which will need to be considered if peace is to be built upon solid foundations. Discussion, debate, and understanding by our people prior to ending of the war are necessary if adequate plans are to be drawn. And the American delegates to the peace table should not only be armed with the principles of peace which America believes workable, but they should have an understanding people behind them.

We may again observe that, if we scan the history of

modern Western civilization, we can see that following long periods of world wars and world disorder, new shapes and new forms of nations have emerged. Civilization has taken on new impulses and new directions. We must expect new forms and new directions from the gigantic explosion beginning in 1914. No one can pretend to see these coming shapes and forms clearly. All that can be known only in the minds and hearts of men and women who live to see those days.

Yet we do know we must make peace when the cheering bugle blows "Cease Firing" at the end of this war. And we know beyond all doubt that the seven dynamic forces will sit at the peace table, as they did in 1919, even though six of them come as unbidden and unwelcome guests. Ideologic, economic, nationalistic, imperialistic, and militaristic pressures, and the witches of fear, hate, and revenge will participate in every discussion.[1] But on the other hand, the prayers of a stricken world for a lasting peace will echo through those halls. The seven dynamic forces have survived every crisis. They will be with us again. We know all this from the nature of the human animal, from his long, toilsome experience.

We propose to discuss the problems which these forces

[1]In describing the seven dynamic forces early in this book, we said: "These forces are not arranged in order of their importance. That varies in different periods. They overlap and are interwoven in the whole fabric of civilization. Other students may prefer different divisions and different designations for these parts of world anatomy. We have reached the conclusion, however, that these divisions and separations most nearly represent not only these dominant world movements but are historically the more conclusive basis and they furnish a new approach in discussion of these problems.

"The history of peace and war is largely a recitation of the operation of these forces and the failures of men to comprehend and control them. Much of it is mistakenly written into terms of personalities both good and bad. Now is the time when the problems of this peace must be studied in far larger patterns than ever before" (p. 11).

will lay upon the next peace table—and to search for some specific deductions, some experience, and some lessons that emerge from the long struggle of humanity to deal with them. We shall suggest some fifty such specific conclusions.

The first of these conclusions is:

1. We have had experience with misunderstanding and divided views on peace aims, such as developed immediately after the Armistice in 1918 despite the Fourteen Points of President Wilson; therefore, before this war ends, the war aims and the principles of peace should be reduced to more specific and more practical terms than those expressed in the Atlantic Declaration of President Roosevelt and Prime Minister Churchill. And there should be agreement now on the methods by which the machinery of peacemaking is to be handled by the United Nations.

The next of these conclusions from experience is:

2. Any structure of lasting peace must consist of two parts. The first is its foundation of political, territorial, military, economic, and ideological settlements which restore order and recovery in the world. The second is the erection thereon of some instrumentality to preserve peace.

The temple where the flame of peace is to be kept will not endure unless the foundations are more deeply and more securely laid than those of Westphalia, Vienna, and Versailles.

On those occasions, strains and pressures of the seven dynamic forces were ignored or only partially allayed, or even increased. The world must now lay those foundations rightly, or any superstructure to preserve peace will fail.

Before we discuss the architecture of the temple itself, we must sift from reason and experience the definite methods which will allay the destructive dynamic strains and will give stability to the world. Here history is positive and experience extended.

We may perhaps be a mite critical that most thought is being devoted to alternative architectural forms of the temple rather than to the foundations. And many who contemplate the nature of the foundations assume that, because the pressure and strains are great and strong, they must be inexorable and little can be done about them. If we enter into the drafting room in this despair, we may as well accept the utter futility of all human efforts to keep the peace.

The authors believe, on the contrary, that a recognition of these forces themselves, together with the lessons to be drawn from experience, does point to avenues of hope for the future.

Ideological Forces

We will first deal with the ideological forces. And we refresh the reader's mind with our early description of this force.

> The importance of religious faith, of social, economic, political, artistic, and scientific ideas in shaping the form of the world and the making of its wars and peace is not to be estimated as less than that of other basic forces. Over the long range of history, they are the determining factors in civilization.
>
> One thing is certain: that is, that the ideas which involve human belief and faith contain a militant crusading spirit. Within them is

inherent aggressiveness. Great and revolutionary ideas have within them at least a period when they are borne aloft by military action. Christianity, the Divine Right of Kings—with all its descendents in the armor of feudalism—Mohammedanism, the Protestant Reformation, and Liberalism have all in their time marched with the sword. Now, new ideologies—Communism, Fascism, and Nazism—are on the warpath. And ideological wars, whether religious or temporal, are more cruel and more bitter than were the wars of mere conquest or exploitation. While the ideology of personal liberty is today less aggressive than the ideologies of collectivism, it can rise to crusading heights.

Ideologists can also make for peace. For these nineteen centuries, Christianity has been unique among religious faiths in its preaching of peace and compassion. Personal liberty and representative government as a political concept have also preached the gospel of peace. Both, at times, have sought to impose their beliefs with the sword. But their final purpose is peace. And as long as men have beliefs, they will strive to protect and expand them (p. 12).

We have before us today certain declared pledges and peace aims in the Atlantic Declaration and other statements of the President. They are in part ideological.

3. Indeed, so far as America is concerned, this war is a crusade for personal liberty against totalitarianism and dictatorship. The direction to destroy these and to substitute personal freedom and representative government "everywhere" has already been assigned to the peacemakers by our expressed purpose in entering the war.

It will be seen from our statement on page 93 that Mr. Roosevelt's announced ideological aims parallel those of Mr. Wilson. President Roosevelt has given added emphasis by his statement of the four "essential freedoms"—"freedom of speech" and "expression," "freedom of worship," "freedom from want," "freedom from fear," "everywhere in the world." Thus, Mr. Roosevelt again states the same major purposes in America's participation in this war—a second crusade to establish American ideals.

Again America asks for no territory; it asks for no indemnities; but this time we want the foundations of peace built on rock and not on sand. The fact that we built on sand last time was partly due to the fact that, during the war, Mr. Wilson contented himself with inspiring generalizations, the meanings of which were differently construed by different nations and differently construed before and after the Armistice. Further than that, no one can review[2] the malign forces which surrounded that peace conference without the conclusion that no such assembly should again be convened. We discuss this at length in Chapter XIV, but at this point we may present our first deduction.

Representative Government as the Foundation of Peace. We believe that the whole experience of the last 100 years as reviewed by this book supports the conviction that the will to peace can genuinely flourish only in the soil of representative government. We do not suggest that it is a perfect guarantee of peace. Nations with representative government are not free from wars. They are capable of military crusades to establish their gospel, and even of imperialistic conquest.

As distinguished, however, from dictatorships and totalitarianism, the aims of representative governments are more generally peaceable. Dictatorships and totalitarianism are in their very nature aggressive, militaristic,

[2]See Chapter VI.

and imperialistic in character. In contrast, personal liberty and representative government can flourish only in peace. The price of war to democracy is the immediate sacrifice of personal freedom and the uncertainty of its recovery. Its price is prolonged impoverishment after the war and infinite grief from loss of its sons. Thus, in representative government, there is always the live voice of opposition and warning against incurring these consequences.

A further proof of the pacific character of representative government is that during the last fifty years the major development of pacific settlement of controversies by international law, international co-operation, mediation, and arbitration, has mostly been at the hands of such nations. In such self-denying agreements as the Kellogg-Briand Pact, based entirely on morals and reason, there has not been a single violation by important representative governments. Moreover, there was no spirit of war or imperialism during the democratic regimes of Germany, Austria, or Hungary.

4. *Our next deduction, therefore, is that the American thesis of 1919, that peace should be built on fostering representative government, was correct, and the best foundation of hope for lasting peace.*

There are some profound lessons to consider, however, in any attempt to force personal liberty and representative government upon other nations.

5. *Ideologies of personal liberty and free will cannot be imposed by machine guns. Wrong ideas cannot be cured by war or by treaty. They are matters of mind and spirit. The lasting acceptance of any governing idea lies deep in*

the mores of races and in their intellectual processes. Liberty does not come like manna from heaven; it must be cultivated from rocky soil with infinite patience and great human toil.

Totalitarianism, on the other hand, can be imposed by terror, execution, and the suppression of any thought except that permitted by the masters. Yet there is an instinctive craving of man for personal freedom. He tasted of its invigorating waters in every civilized nation during the last century.

If we were wise enough in the peacemaking, we might start the rebuilding of freedom in some form. Probably not in our exact forms, for every race moves in the orbit of its own mores. But here is the hope of the world. If it can have a reasonable opportunity, freedom will rise again. While personal liberty and representative government, with all their social and economic forms, cannot be imposed, it is a certainty that they cannot even start to grow unless one minimum foundation is laid.

6. Our deduction from all experience is that at least the forms of representative government must be accepted by the enemy states if we are to have lasting peace. Moreover, unless the representatives of a people accept the terms, there can be no lasting peace.

But that alone is not enough. Personal liberty and representative government are a delicate growth. At the end of the last war, the victors set up, or encouraged the setting up, of such governments. But instead of nursing them through their infancy, we allowed them to disintegrate. In some cases, indeed, the older representative governments by their attitudes destroyed them.

7. Therefore, if we want the principle of representative government to prevail, we must make up our minds now to make such a peace as will not only initiate it but nurture it in the enemy states for long years to come.

Economic Forces

We defined the economic forces in Chapter I:

> While we have no faith in theories of complete economic determinism in history, yet they occupy a large place among these seven forces. Since men must have food and living, the striving for them creates external economic forces and pressures.
>
> Certainly, through the history of modern civilization, economic forces have played a large part. It was the wealth of the Indies which stimulated the great explorations and conquests of the fifteenth and sixteenth centuries. Pressures of overpopulation to find outlets for men and goods play a striking part on the world stage today. The cravings for security of supply of raw materials and places to sell surplus products have led to incessant friction, hate, fear, and war. Insistence that "trade follows the flag" has cost rivers of blood and untold sorrow. All these are part of the incentives to imperialism.
>
> Whatever may have been the weight of economic pressures in creating the World War of 1914, the economic aftermaths of that war were among the primary causes of the collapse of the world into this second World War. War's disruption of economic life has been burned into the consciousness of nations, yet not so deeply as was hoped by some observers. But economic forces have also in other times and other circumstances acted as a restraint on war (p. 13).

The relief from economic pressures which make for war is one of the greatest of all problems that must be solved by the peace.

Experience of the last war and its aftermath proves

that these problems fall into two categories. One is the instant problem which arises from the disruption of war. The other is the long-range problem of rebuilding prosperity in the world.

INSTANT ECONOMIC PROBLEMS. Famine and pestilence will be rampant over most of Europe and Asia. Agriculture has already degenerated under war pressures in all parts of Europe. And added to that is the suffering from the blockade and the German seizures. Millions of women and children in the occupied democracies are already sickening and dying. With the disorder and collapse of discipline that will follow upon defeat, there will come the weakening of the rationing systems and distribution of what food there is in the enemy countries. The farmers and villagers and those who can pay black-market prices will get the food, and the poor of the cities will be worse off than they were before the Armistice. To create any sort of order and maintain it pending reconstruction, at least as much food will be needed immediately as after the last war. The volume of relief pending the establishment of normal production and trade will probably exceed 30,000,000 tons of overseas imports of concentrated food.

We have already described (p. 111) how, despite American protests, the blockade of enemy states was continued for months after the last armistice. And it was continued until anarchy and bolshevism had broken out in a dozen centers.

8. Our certain deduction from the last experience is that unless food blockade is instantly removed when firing ceases and the enemy surrenders his military strength, and unless extensive and instant relief is undertaken to enemy and friend alike, there will be no hope of stability in governments upon which peace can be built, and no allaying of war hates.

The immediate economic demoralizations from this present war are likely to be even greater than those of the last war. The world financial exchanges and currencies will be greatly dislocated. Industry will need to be furnished with raw materials to get employment started again. Nations will be without resources with which to buy either food or raw material. Thus, there will be a period where private enterprise and private charity will be totally unable to meet the situation.

9. *We conclude, therefore, that the governments of the world must bear the burdens of shipping, credit, and distribution of supplies. And they will have to bear these burdens for the enemy as well as for liberated countries if there is to be peace and recovery.*

Long-view Economic Problems. International economic relations are obviously the exchange of goods and services. That was the basis of prewar international economy and will be the basis of postwar economy. Any action by governments is merely the stimulation or retarding of exchanges. The longer-view economic problems of peacemaking will be, first, to start the forces in motion by which economic recovery can be attained, and, second, to turn future economic pressures away from war and toward lasting peace.

The problems of reconstruction will in themselves be gigantic. War destruction, the imperative need to return armies and war industries to civilian employment, will present huge problems in every country, whether victor or vanquished. Every nation will be impoverished. Inflation will be in action, for the national debts will be far more enormous than after the first World War. Every country will be in domestic financial disorder.

Moreover, the stock of goods will have been more exhausted than in the last war. Even the scrap and waste will have been mopped up and used. The standards of living will have been reduced greatly in every country before the war ends—even where there still is food and clothing—and the people will be clamoring for resumption of work and living. And they will be demanding haste.

The major problems of economic recovery will arise inside the boundaries of each country. Lasting peace will greatly depend upon such recovery, but those problems go too far afield for this essay. Domestic recovery will, however, be effected by international action—somewhat proportionate to each country's dependence upon foreign trade. In that particular, the United States, with its dependence of only 7 per cent of its national economy on foreign trade, is the most fortunate of all the large countries. Nevertheless, there are most important phases of long-view peace involved which affect recovery of all nations.

The long-range economic tasks of the peace table will be concerned chiefly with the international phases of trade, credit, and currency. Their successful solution affects not only domestic recoveries in the world, but will reduce the economic pressures which militate against lasting peace.

Before we can make deductions from experience as to these problems, we must determine the ideological approach to them. As we have said, for an emergency period these international functions of commodity supplies, shipping, credit, and monetary exchanges will need to be in the hands of governments. That is, of course, a continuation of the totalitarian war economy, partly Fascist, partly Socialist, which is being established in every country as a necessity of war organization.

The ideological question is, will the peacemakers set up a system which will continue this regime beyond the emergency? Or will they set the stage for the return of international economy to private enterprise as fast as it can be taken over? Or will they set the stage to preserve a mixed economy, partly free enterprise, partly totalitarian?

This query rises more insistently because the peace aims so far declared do not include the "Fifth Freedom" —that is, economic freedom.

FREE ENTERPRISE IN INTERNATIONAL TRADE. A number of books and addresses otherwise intelligent upon the problems of lasting peace are yet founded upon the advocacy of some sort of collectivist world economy. It would be ironic that a war for freedom should end in such a defeat of personal liberty.

We must explore these questions further, for they relate, first, to freedom of men (the declared purpose of this war), and, second, to lasting peace. If the purpose of world reconstruction is to give freedom to men, then the return of direction toward economic freedom is essential. We may repeat again:

> To be free, men must choose their callings, bargain for their own services, save and provide for their families and old age. And they must be free to engage in enterprise so long as each does not injure his fellow man. And that requires laws to prevent abuse.

And when we use the terms "Fifth Freedom," "economic freedom," or "free enterprise," we use them in this sense only, not in the sense of *laissez faire* or capitalistic exploitation.

Such freedom does not mean going back to abuses. It in no way inhibits social reforms and social advancement. Economic freedom furnishes the resources for such advancement and flourishes only with such advances.

We have elsewhere touched upon the economic consequences involved in the mixture of totalitarian economic systems into free enterprise under the term "managed economy." We pointed out that the danger to free men arises if the expansion of government over economic life reaches the point where it slows down initiative and enterprise and where centralization and bureaucratization of power encroach upon the safeguards of liberty. The further danger is the inherent spirit of bureaucracy, which makes it seek for more and more power. The problem is somewhat a matter of degree, for at some point along this road economic freedom collapses. Intellectual and spiritual freedom will not long survive the passing of economic freedom. The question becomes insistent because we must move more and more into these dangerous fields in order to win the war.

It would be ironical if, having fought a war to establish freedom, we should have fastened any form of collectivism on our own country.

The transcendent thing in ideological forces is the direction in which they are moving, and that depends upon our ultimate aims.

10. In our view, the ideals of freedom, national unity during the war, economic recovery after the war, and lasting peace all require a strong reassurance now that the ideals and objectives of the war include economic freedom regulated to prevent abuse. Such a determination is vital if the hopes, confidence and initiative of men are to survive.

As we said above, these questions of economic freedom bear not only upon the restoration of freedom itself. The direction that we take determines the method of handling economic problems at the peace table, and it affects the whole question of lasting peace.

For instance, under any form of economy, when governments engage in exchange of commodities, or credit or financial controls, or in the conduct of shipping, they become higglers in the market with other governments. Thus, all the natural conflicts and frictions of the market as to price, quantity, credit, and a thousand other things become conflicts and frictions between governments. When governments engage in these activities, they become competitors with other governments in world markets, both to buy scarce materials and to sell surpluses. Under private traders, such activities do not involve governments, and thereby avoid centralizing their cumulative effects into national emotions. Moreover, government trading also involves the creation of domestic conflicts within their own borders. Agriculture, labor, and industry bring pressures to bear on government, on legislatures and administration to advance their special interests—and all these pressures become political in character.

11. We believe the whole experience of the last twenty years of government trading in commodities, credit, and shipping has demonstrated that it is alive with international friction and threats to peace. And therefore, from the standpoint of lasting peace, the long view should be to restore international trade to free enterprise.

12. There also enters the fact that international economy must be a reflection of domestic economy. International economic freedom cannot function if there is to be a degree of domestic managed economy which stifles free enterprise, for then there would be no substantial force behind private trading, and governments must take over.

Nor can there be domestic economic freedom parallel with government international trading, for free enterprise could not survive against the power of governments in international trade.

CHAPTER XI

The Foundations of Lasting Peace

(Continued)

Economic Forces

(Continued)

Bulking large in public discussions today are the reduction of trade barriers after the war, freedom of supply in raw materials, and freedom of the seas. These are indeed essential for economic recovery.

Trade Barriers. In order of importance, there are six varieties of the barriers to trade:

1. Governmental buying and selling.
2. Unstable currencies.
3. Special agreements, such as reciprocal treaties and preferential agreements.
4. Quotas.
5. Monopolies and cartels.
6. Tariffs.

Most of these practices, except tariffs, were the product of the demoralization from the first World War. Each frantic to secure its own recovery, all nations drove toward self-containment under the pressures of unemployment or demoralization of credit and currency and markets or the recollection of the privations imposed during the war by shortage in shipping and the blockade.

GOVERNMENT BUYING AND SELLING. As to governmental buying and selling, solely in their economic aspects, it may be said at once that the whole process is restrictive to volume in the movement of trade. It is, therefore, a barrier to trade. It is only the efforts of a multitude of individuals and of enterprises, seeking every opening for production and sale, that can move the maximum of goods. Bureaucrats, hampered by the red tape of governments, cannot find or create the maximum, either of supplies or markets.

13. In any event, if there is to be a restoration of a real volume of international trade, there must be assurance of ultimate removal of all government buying and selling in foreign markets except for possible storage of raw materials for international stabilization, to which we refer later.

Moreover, if governments are to conduct trading, there is no need to worry over trade barriers. The very assumption of removal of barriers implies free enterprise because barriers are questions of private trading, not trading by governments. In government trading, barriers are replaced by barter.

UNSTABLE CURRENCIES. Next to government trading, probably the worst of all barriers to the growth of trade is to be found in unstable currencies. The failure to secure monetary stability after the last war was a major contribution to the economic disaster of the world and added impulse to the revolt from liberalism.

The whole question of stability of currency is greatly involved with credits, but credits are not the whole problem. When a nation devalues its currency, it, in effect, increases its tariffs. After the American devaluation of the dollar in 1933, the American people had to pay more dollars for British or other foreign goods. Theoretically, it was an increase equivalent to a raise of more than 100 per cent in the tariff. Its effect was at once to stifle imports. Similarly, the repeated devaluations in foreign countries had the same effect of stifling exports to them. Of equally great importance is that any fluctuation or uncertainty of currencies creates a wide hazard for merchants, which they must cover with higher prices.

The universal introduction of governmentally managed currencies since the last war presents a huge problem. Dependent as they are upon bureaucratic action for their value, the hazard of uncertainty at once enters into trade. Moreover, experience proves that such currencies inevitably become a nationalistic device to influence the movement of goods. In so doing, they create a mass of barriers to trade in themselves.

It may be that the world's solution over 6,000 years by the use of gold convertibility to give stability to currency and to enable the settlement of international balances is, after all, the only device humanity has found which will serve these purposes.

It is impossible to create currency and credit stability by loaning America's hoard of gold to other governments. They would at once send the gold back to us in exchange for our commodities. There is no reason in all experience to believe that they would repay the loans. We would simply be giving presents of our commodities and labor and we should have the unjust impoverishment of more Americans. The real solution is to distribute this gold hoard by the purchase of foreign goods of the types which we do not produce in sufficiency—and thereby enrich both buyer and seller.

14. Experience shows that this problem of monetary stability must be taken up at the peace table. We should begin again the work of the economic conference instigated by Mr. Hoover in 1933, where the combined resources and co-operative policies of all nations were to be brought to bear. It must be solved by calling upon the resources of all nations, not of America alone.

Solution of the co-related credit problem will probably have to be found through some sort of credit pool in which all nations pledge their resources. In this problem it will be necessary to examine the possibility of using a reserve of raw materials to be created in times of lower prices and depressions as an adjunct to international credit and currency stabilization.

SPECIAL TRADE AGREEMENTS. The whole essence of reciprocal trade agreements—whether by tariffs or other devices—results in the creation of special favor or trade between a few nations.

The effect of reciprocal tariff agreements is somewhat modified by the "most favored nation clause." But all nations do not have the benefit of that arrangement. It must be said, in support of Mr. Hull's efforts in this regard, that reciprocal agreements by America were mostly for the purpose of lowering the American tariff. But from the point of view of world trade as a whole, most of the governments at the other end of these agreements were moved by special advantage to themselves.

There is another type of special trade agreements among certain nations which seek sheer discrimination and privilege against others. These are at once a barrier to free movement of world trade. After the last war, the whole world set to work spinning this particular web of barriers to trade. It was one reason for retarded recovery everywhere.

15. All special trade agreements which establish privilege between either two nations or groups should be abolished.

Quotas. One of the worst of all human inventions in trade barriers is the quota. That invention, discovered since the last war, is a complete wall against trade, with doors open only to favored nations and in favored amounts. It sums up to a 10,000 per cent tariff with a special privilege attachment. Quotas, plus special agreements, have been developed by the totalitarian nations into a practical control of the foreign trade of some other nations.

16. All quotas everywhere in the world should be abolished.

Monopolies and Cartels. Monopolies and cartels created within a nation or between nations at once reach into control of prices and distribution of goods to other nations. They are again a vicious barrier to trade and they enter into the problem of access to raw materials which we discuss later.

17. All monopolies and cartels which limit foreign trade should be prohibited by the peace.

TARIFFS. The old-fashioned tariffs—which have existed for 2,000 years—can be serious barriers to trade. They, however, occupy an exaggerated importance in public discussion as compared to these other barriers. And unlike the other barriers developed mostly since the last war, they are, through centuries of universal use in all countries, deeply imbedded in the economy of nations. They are not easy to deal with. In the first instance, we can be sure they will be continued upon luxury goods as a necessary source of government revenues. And the definition of luxury goods varies somewhat with every country.

The roots of the protective principle as distinguished from revenue lie in its use by every democracy to safeguard their workmen and farmers from goods produced under lower standards of living and longer hours of work. This protection will be hard to move, because industries, cities, schools, churches, and skills have been built under these walls.

Total war has also added new impulses for the use of tariffs as a protective device as well as all the other barriers. During the last war and in this war, many neutral nations were, and are, deprived of essential goods by inability to secure supplies from belligerents either because of shortage of shipping or diversion of production by belligerents to their own use. In consequence, when Argentine children were unable, during the last war, to attend school because shoes could not be had, it is not surprising that Argentina proceeded to nurture a domestic shoe industry by protective devices. The nations which, before the first World War, were dependent upon imports of food, clothing, and other necessities, found themselves reduced to great suffering by blockade and shipping shortages; in consequence, they resolutely stimulated their own agriculture through tariffs as a primary defense measure. Another impulse to protective tariffs of the same sort arises from the synthetic raw-material industries upon which nations have desperately expended billions for defense supplies, such as rubber, chemicals, and minerals. They will want to retain these defenses. Another impulse arises from the breakdown of credit for foreign purchases in the after-war economic demoralization. It again drives towards self-containment through trade barriers.

The probability is that if protective tariffs had not been invented prior to the World War of 1914, they would have been invented afterwards. In any event, after the last war, a large number of nations established tariffs or increased them prior to the general American increase of 1931. It will take a long period of peace and order to allay these fears and restore confidence that foreign supplies can always be obtained. The tariffs will be a harder nut to crack than the other barriers. The most practical thing to do is probably to place tariffs on a basis of reasonable competition between imports and domestic production and, above all, have them equal to all nations. That was first attempted in the United States through the flexible tariff provisions based upon relative cost of production at home and abroad and determined by a non-political body. If every country adopted such principles, the worst of the tariff question would disappear.

TARIFFS. The United States has always been the world's whipping boy on tariffs. Yet all the major nations in the world have maintained tariffs against us from the day we became an independent people. And after Versailles, fifty-seven of them increased their tariffs before the upward revision by the American Congress in 1931. World trade would undoubtedly be benefited by reduction of this barrier, but we need some clear thinking as to how it can be accomplished. There is a widespread and mistaken notion that unilateral self-denying action by the United States would suffice to solve the problem. As a matter of fact such action would merely place us in a disadvantageous position, deprived of bargaining power. If tariff barriers are to be effectively reduced, all nations must act simultaneously.

18. For world recovery and world good will, tariffs certainly require two restraints: first, that they be equal to all nations; second, that they be no higher than will preserve fair competition of imports with domestic production.

Furthermore, both experience and common sense declare that all forms of trade barriers—whether governmental buying and selling, unstable currencies, reciprocal agreements, preferences, quotas, monopolies, cartels, or excessive tariffs—must have vigorous overhauling in the next peace. Certainly, if there is to be relief from trade barriers, there must be equal rights and no discrimination between nations and no agreements should be permitted that are not open equally to all nations.

ACCESS TO RAW MATERIALS. Access to raw materials has also loomed large in public discussion and is often prescribed as a panacea for both political and economic peace. Few of those who prescribe it realize its origin. This cry was originally raised by Germany and became one of the cornerstones of her propaganda for return of her colonies. And in this propaganda, the Germans originated the cry of the "have" and "have not" nations. The "have not" nations we heard about were always Germany, Italy, and Japan. Yet no nation produces all of its own raw materials—not even the United States or Great Britain. They are also "have nots" in the sense of this argument. But they have somehow contrived during peace to trade with other nations for ample supplies of their deficient raw materials.

All this agitation has tended to create an illusion in the world that raw materials have a direct relation to lasting peace and an acceptance of the idea that a great problem exists somewhere in this connection. We believe the importance of the problem is entirely overestimated from an international point of view.

19. The economic fact is that there have always been and are ample raw material supplies available to any nation during peace if they will produce the goods to exchange for them. Too often, nations have consumed materials and labor in making arms and munitions that otherwise could be converted into goods that could be exchanged for raw materials.

That there are ample supplies is indicated by the fact that the energies of many governments have been devoted to restricting production of rubber, wheat, sugar, coffee, cotton, nitrate, potash, tin, oil, coal, and fats and fibers in order to hold a living price for the producers of these commodities. There are large reserves of raw material in the world which are undeveloped because they will not provide wages of a decent standard of living or a return upon the capital needed. If, at any time, the world is prepared to pay a little larger price, further supplies are available.

And chemistry is also rapidly solving the question of imported raw materials. Nitrates and light metals can now be produced in every country. Oil, rubber, and textiles are on their way.

As to price, many raw materials have been sold over long terms of years—all but boom years—at less than the real cost of production to the exporting nation. That is particularly the case in more speculative products, such as oil, copper, lead, zinc, tin, and other nonferrous metals. In these speculative industries, some ventures are profitable, but in many there is total loss, and these losing ventures are not included in the costs and prices of the successful ones.

Agricultural raw materials are obviously in ample supply and at reasonable prices, and, except in wartime, their prices do not, over long periods, produce for the farmer as high a standard of living as that of the mechanic.

There have been cases of onerous restrictions on price or supply of raw materials beyond a mere desire for decent living standards through monopoly controls, such as the British rubber and tin controls, the German potash, the Dutch quinine cartels, and the international steel control. These obstructions have to be abolished.

In war, of course, the control of raw-material supply becomes a military weapon. The cry for "equality in raw materials" is partly a cry that comes from a desire for assured war supplies. The inequality of the "haves" and the "have nots" is vivid enough then.

If anything is meant by the discussion of this subject other than equal rights for all citizens of all nations to purchase raw materials of the world, then it reaches into questions of sovereignty over such materials. This sort of "access" question is, in reality, a nationalist and military question, not an economic one, and is a matter of satisfying the national spirit. Nations do like to have sovereignty over areas of raw materials so that they may have an outlet for population, for skills, and satisfactions of national pride—a place in the sun. It also gives still more assurance of supplies in war. In these practical phases, this becomes a question of colonies. But even a redistribution of colonies would not provide everybody with raw materials. Anyone familiar with their distribution in the world would realize that to give parts of all the different raw-material areas to everybody is wholly impossible. That would not be limited to colonies but would disintegrate nations. Would we consider giving copper and oil to Britain or Germany by ceding a part of Montana or of Texas? Are we going to claim parts of Russia or Brazil which contain manganese?

20. The whole experience of the past hundred years shows that the assurance of supplies of raw materials requires only a dissolution of monopoly controls, an assurance of equal prices, open markets—and peace.

Immigration. Another difficult phase of economic pressures to be allayed if we are to have lasting peace is the problem of elbow room for expanding and virile peoples. There is also a problem in refuge for minorities.

The problem is, however, one which involves questions of racial identity, of cultural prejudices, spiritual unity, competitive economic standards of life, and many other difficulties. It must be approached realistically. There is no such thing possible as free immigration. Every self-governing nation is going to determine what sort of people it will admit through its boundaries. It will certainly continue to prevent the ingress of people mentally deficient, diseased, criminal, illiterate, or likely to become a public charge. It can hardly be expected that the Western governments will permit indiscriminate and unlimited immigration. This is not a matter of racial prejudice. The objection is on quite other grounds. Some of these races, notably those of Asia, are trained by a hundred generations to eat less, wear less, seek less shelter, and work longer hours than any Western race can endure. No Western standards can compete with them in their midst. Nor should nations with great unemployment be asked to support floods of unemployed from other quarters.

21. The constructive thing is to direct the streams of immigration toward undeveloped countries. The whole requires a definite plan of preparation which should be taken up at the peace table. There are large suitable areas in South America and Africa.

We shall make a suggestion upon this subject later.

FREEDOM OF THE SEAS. The freedom of the seas as a problem of peace is a much overestimated issue. During peace, except for the rare revival of old-fashioned piracy, there has been no consequential interference with free movement of merchant ships for a century or more.

The question is wholly one of freedom of the seas during war. And that revolves around the blockade measures of belligerents. With the modern development of blockade in total war, there is no freedom of the seas in war. Even trade between neutrals is controlled by the belligerents through pressures upon their coal and other supplies and blacklists upon merchants.

However, this question has agitated the world for centuries, and a vast amount of international agreement and international law has been built around the definition of blockade and the rights of neutrals in respect to it.

President Wilson, in the second of his Fourteen Points of January 1918, gave probably the most complete formula covering the question that has yet been made. He proposed:

> Absolute freedom of navigation upon the seas outside territorial waters alike in peace and in war, except as the seas may be closed in whole or in part by international action for the enforcement of international covenants.

This proposal was rejected by the British Government in November 1918, and received no consideration at the Versailles Peace Conference.

On September 11, 1941, President Roosevelt, speaking of the long-established American policy of freedom of the seas, said:

> It means that no nation has the right to make the broad oceans of the world at great distances from the actual theater of war unsafe for the commerce of others.

In the Churchill-Roosevelt declaration of August 1941, it is said:

> Such a peace should enable all men to traverse the high seas and oceans without hindrance.

However, this expression applies only to peace and, therefore, does not solve the real problem which is during war.

22. Just and humane rules of the sea during war should again be revived. The rights of neutrals should again be established. They could no doubt be made to hold in secondary wars. But if total war is to be a part of the calendar of humanity, they have little hope of use in such wars except so far as they hold by fear of reprisals. Nevertheless, such standards should again be erected in the world, and President Wilson's formula is the most effective starting point.

There is one segment of freedom of the seas, of vast importance to humanity, which should be worked out and might be so set that it would hold even in total war.

The food blockade has proved to be an endless chain of brutality, fear, hate, revenge, reprisals, and stimulation to armament. It should be stopped if there is to be any hope of lasting peace. A large part of naval building arises from the determination of nations to protect their overseas food supplies and to deprive the enemy of them.

Total war in 1914 brought the extension of food blockade to whole nations. In that war, blockade of civilian food by the Allies contributed a secondary factor only to the defeat of Germany and Austria. That defeat was brought about by armies. The countersubmarine blockade of England even at that time came perilously near to defeating her, but for American intervention. The food blockade does not deprive government officials, soldiers, and munition workers. They have a priority and are always fed. The burden falls upon women, children, and the infirm. Those mutual food blockades, with the stunting of children on one side and ruthless killing of sailors on the other, left hate indelibly imprinted on generations in both peoples.

Germany and her allies, having had the experience of the first World War, prepared for the present war by intensifying agriculture and building up stocks. Today

Britain is experiencing at least as much danger and suffering from the submarine and air blockade as is Germany from surface craft. The day is gone when the food blockade is a worth-while weapon in war.

The physical and spiritual degeneration from it will last another generation. It is all a futility and a brutal folly.

In 1929, Mr. Hoover proposed a remedy. That was to vest the overseas food supply of all combatants in the hands of the combined neutrals, to be delivered in full cargo lots, the ships to be free from attack on both sides. The plan was welcomed at that time by the great majority of nations, but rejected by a few, who prevented unanimity. It had been tried in a practical way in the first World War and saved the Belgians.

It is true, agreements making for more humane war survive only through fear of reprisals and fear of neutral opinion. This plan would invoke both, and neutrals would be interested not only in the humane aspects, but in keeping their markets open.

With the again proven experience of the almost equal futility of the surface blockade against the Axis and the submarine blockade against the British to produce anything but damage to the health of women, children, and aged of both nations, it would seem that now the fear of reprisals would uphold such an agreement. Certainly, the first to violate such agreement would incur the denunciation of every decent person in the world.

23. *We believe such action should be taken in the peace, for it would lessen brutality, minimize the incentives to build great navies, and open to the world a new hope of lessened hate and revenge.*

CHAPTER XII

The Foundations of Lasting Peace

(Concluded)

NATIONALISM

AS WE STATED in Chapter I:

Nationalism has developed from the deepest of primitive instincts and emotional forces in mankind.

It gathers from a thousand springs of common race with its common language, religion, folklore, traditions, literature, art, music, beliefs, habits, modes of expression, hates, fears, ideals, and tribal loyalties. It expresses itself in patriotism, which is itself built from the fundamentals of love of family, love of country, pride in racial accomplishments. Men fight for their hearths and their homes. They fight for their flag.

From all these racial instincts and mores rises the eternal yearning for independence from foreign subjection or domination. Thus, the subjection of races is one of the most potent of all causes of war. Nations are eternally striving for independence—self-determination. The oppressions which they suffer harden their souls and invigorate their resistance. All the thousands of years of human history are punctuated by wars of independence. . . .

Nationalism will not be stilled by battle or defeat. It is fired to greater heat by every war and every peacemaking. A fiercer nationalism flares out of every defeat and every victory.

Victorious peoples who have marched to the defense of their homes and country to the stirring words of their national songs, who have followed their flags on the battlefield, who have sacrificed their sons and their wealth are little inclined to accept abrogation of their independence of action or of their sovereignty.

Nationalism can be both a cause of war or a bulwark of peace and progress. The values of nationalism cannot be ignored because of its secondary evils.

Where it is an impulse to strive for independence from oppression, for defense against aggression, it makes for war. But independence and spiritual unity, pride of country, constructive rivalry, the building of national cultures out of cohesive mores, the better conduct of government in areas of unity of thought and purpose bring more flowering of progress and the expansion of cultural institutions, scientific research, art, music, and literature. Nationalism, in the best sense, is a satisfaction, a fulfillment.

Extreme nationalism does have liabilities to peace and progress. As among individuals, there are ambitions in races for glory and for power of the race. Dignity, honor, and aggrandizement of his country is a satisfaction to the individual. To gain a place in the sun is an inspiring call.

Nationalism can readily expand into dangerous forms—greed in exploitation of the resources and foreign trade of other peoples and in aggression which quickly runs into imperialism.

There are about sixty separate nations in the world. And in the deep currents of human emotion, the primary interest of every citizen of them is his own country, first and foremost.

Nationalism, with all its emotions, will continue as long as man inhabits this earth and will have to be embraced in any plan to preserve the peace [p. 13].

Nationalism, being fed with the earliest milk to every human animal, will not be stamped out by this war. It will continue as it has continued since the dawn of civilization. It will be even more heated after the sacrifices of this war.

SMALL NATIONS. We Americans, through "self-determination" and "self-government" of nations, were pledged to sustain the theory of nationalism in the last World War. This sprang from our desire to see men free from oppression. Fifteen new nations sprang into independence from that victory. We have renewed those pledges in this war—and more new nations will spring to independence, or at least self-government, at the peace.

Success has expanded Japanese ideas to embrace the hegemony of one billion Asiatics, controlling, molding, and pitting them against the Western World. No other Asiatic race of consequence possesses a skilled military class. The others can be depended upon to pursue peace if freed from this domination and leadership. But upon that defeat, other problems of Asia will arise to meet our pledges of independence and self-government. The self-government of India is assured by the British undertaking to establish Commonwealth status. But Burma, Indo-China, the Malay States, and the peoples of the Dutch Indies will also be asserting their claims to independence. It would seem unlikely that the American people will wish to sacrifice their sons to restore them to subjection. That would be repugnant to our whole national ideal.

Moreover, we have pledged ourselves "to restore sovereign rights and self-government to those who have been forcibly deprived of them." That pledge will demand restoration of the independence of the Norwegians, the French, the Danes, the Finns, the Estonians, the Latvians, the Lithuanians, the Poles, the Czechs, the Slovaks, the

Slovenes, the Croats, the Serbs, the Greeks, the Albanians, the Dutch, the Belgians, the Luxemburgers, the Koreans, the Ethiopians, the Persians, the Arabs, the Siamese, and the Filipinos. In any event, the moment the enemy's power crumbles and the bugle of victory sounds, they will instantly resume their own governments.

They will wait for no peacemakers to act upon the needs of their peoples. Their economic, boundary and defense policies will present great problems.

24. All these nations and peoples of Europe and Asia will insist upon their independence and their own cultures. To deny them will bring no lasting peace. But there must need be better organization of them if they are to keep the peace.

The problem lies in finding methods of averting so far as possible the elements of conflict that arose from the creation of many new countries at the end of the last war. These countries must come to the peace table for recognition of their independence, or at least for necessary political and financial assistance, which amounts to much the same thing. This affords a fleeting opportunity to exercise a restraining influence.

We have seen that unrest and suspicion were increased in Europe by the way in which the multitude of new states hedged themselves about with economic barriers; by their building up of military forces and the making of military alliances which gave concern to their neighbors; and by their difficulties with their racial minorities. These three problems must be examined separately.

Many of these smaller eastern European states are in reality part of larger natural economic areas. Such is the case of the states in the Danube Valley—Czechoslovakia,

Austria, Yugoslavia, and Hungary. From every standpoint of raw materials, complementary agriculture, manufactures, and transportation, they should be in one economic unit. After the last war, the barriers they set up against one another impoverished them all. There are other economic unifications which would make for prosperity and lessened friction, and thereby for more lasting peace.

At the end of the last war, all the newly independent countries set about building up strong armies and making military combinations and alliances. This meant not only that they were living beyond their means and making full recovery impossible; it also meant that they were causing suspicion and apprehension in neighboring countries and encouraging them in turn to increase their armed forces. These alliances proved worthless in any event.

25. History has shown us that the possession of highly developed armed forces by small nations is disastrous in all its consequences. These forces do not suffice for successful defense against a powerful enemy. They serve for the most part as a real or fancied provocation, and eventually lead to military disaster.

The problem of irredentas also plagued these small states, for minorities were included which they could neither absorb nor control. We mention this further later on, as it concerns larger states as well.

It may be that there is a lesson to be learned by the smaller nations of Europe from the history of Switzerland. Here three divergent races grouped in a cantonal government with a very great cantonal autonomy have dwelt in peace among themselves and in independence for centuries. Switzerland has always been a force for peace.

There were, of course, certain factors which favored the success of the Swiss experiment. But the fact remains that the Swiss have set up a small country composed of several races with different languages and traditions, and that by the exercise of tolerance and local government they have succeeded. If they had acted according to the methods current elsewhere in Europe, they would have had an Italian, and perhaps a French, irredenta. For centuries they have avoided this mistake and probably thereby averted the destruction of their country. Perhaps the secret of their success is that they accorded equal rights to all racial elements regardless of their importance in percentages of population.

It was the original intention at the Paris Peace Conference that Czechoslovakia should be organized on the Swiss model. Indeed, this was proposed in writing by Dr. Beneš. It is perhaps too much to hope that some sort of cantonal, federated, or economic unions be set up in these areas.

26. Certainly, the experience of history, and notably of the last peace, would seem to show at least the desirability of making the independence of these small countries conditional upon their accepting certain definite undertakings to refrain from building up the sort of economic barriers and military action which contributed so powerfully to their own collapse and the collapse in Europe after the last war.

IRREDENTAS. The nations of Europe will be faced with problems of mixed populations on their borders.

27. Bitter experience for a hundred years shows that these European irredentas are a constant source of war.

Consideration should be given even to the heroic remedy of transfer of populations.

The hardship of moving is great, but it is less than the constant suffering of minorities and the constant recurrence of war. The action involved in most cases is less drastic than the transfer of the Greeks and the Turks after the last war—and the lessening of tension brought about by that transfer measurably improved both the prosperity and amity of the two nations. A careful study should, of course, be made as to the possibility of real and final remedy.

GERMAN UNITY. A still larger question of nationalism will arise over Germany. Any survey of the history of Europe will show that, in its periodic defeats, this race has been dismembered into separate states.

There is a widespread feeling that a united Germany constitutes a menace to peace and that the obvious solution lies in dividing the country and keeping it divided—at least isolating the Prussians who have provided the motive power for repeated aggressions. Advocacy of this proposal is described as being realistic.

Before committing ourselves to such a course we should try to satisfy ourselves as to whether it is realistic. The Germans, like all virile races, are cohesive. The incubation of movements for unity has usually exploded a European war. That was the case in 1866, 1870, and 1939. The more realistic interpretation is that it is the division of Germany that feeds her militarism and breeds wars.

Another test of dismemberment proposals is whether the solution could be maintained. In other words, can we be confident that the United Nations, once they have imposed a partition of Germany, will maintain for all time an identity of interest and purpose among themselves and be at all times prepared to exert their united strength to prevent by force any movement toward German unity? We find nothing in history to justify any such hope. During a great war allied nations are held together by a common peril and a common purpose. Once the peril is past and the common purpose achieved, conflicts of interests come to the fore. And dismembered Germany uses and widens these conflicts of interest in her efforts toward unity. Within a few years after Versailles the identity of interest disappeared and the carefully prepared measures for holding Germany down not only lost all their efficacy but resulted in ferment over all Europe.

Change of relationships among governments is one of the few things that are certain in international affairs. We should therefore be on our guard against assuming that we can establish a new *status quo* to our own taste opposed to living forces and then maintain it indefinitely.

28. There can be no lasting peace in Europe with a dismembered Germany, any more than there could be a lasting peace in North America if other nations tried to separate the states or to put parts of them under Mexico. In the light of historical experience, the sound course is to give the Germans an incentive for abandoning their old ways and becoming a peaceful nation.

Imperialism

We said in Chapter I:

> Another of the larger forces moving in all history is imperialism. It may, for our purposes, be defined as the movement of races over their racial borders.

It is part cause, part effect. It springs from excessive nationalism, militarism, thirst for power, and economic pressures. They all feed upon one another. Old as the Chaldeans and as modern as this morning, its purpose has not changed, although its form has altered. At one time, part of the motivation of imperialism was dynastic or racial glory; at another, zeal to spread religious faith—for instance, Mohammedanism or Christianity. But in modern civilization, its motivation has been chiefly economic.

Modern imperialism has developed into three varieties, of which one is justified by modern moral standards, the second may be justified, and the third has no justification in morals or hope of peace. The first variety is expansion of races into the settlement and development of areas mostly unpopulated; the second, into areas of uncivilized races incapable of self-government; the third, sheer conquest of civilized races. The last two have always embodied one purpose—that is, to secure superior living by exploiting other races and their resources.

Whether its impelling force be glory, prestige, spread of religion, ideology, development of backward races, or exploitation of labor and resources, imperialism is not essentially an appendage of the Divine Right of Kings or the attribute of dictators. Democracies have been no less imperialistic than kings, emporers, or dictators. Rome was imperialistic before the Emperor was invented. Britain and France and the United States have expanded steadily. But wherever imperialism has been successful over long periods, it has always rested upon class government.

There can be no doubt that domination and exploitation of other races is one of the eternal causes of war. We know of no case where it has made for durable peace. Even in the phase of expansion over backward races or into open spaces, the rivalries between imperialisms have made for war. In the spread of civilization, it has compensations. But as a method of advancing peace, it cannot be given a great deal of credit. Much can be said for a satiated empire like Britain, which has arrived at a point where it becomes a stabilizing force. More especially that Empire, being liberal in instinct, makes for representative government among its components.

But imperialism as a theory of maintaining peace in the modern world has the disturbing consequence of setting up a dozen rival forms of Pax Romana to fight one another [p. 17].

The war-perpetuating monster, imperialism, is present in this war in a large way—and it will be present at the peace table as well. It was greatly weakened in the last war by freeing thirteen nations from Germany, Austria, Russia, and Turkey. It gained some strength through territories acquired by Britain, Italy, France, and Japan. But with victory for the United Nations in this war, Germany, Italy, and Japan should be finally cured of imperialism through restoration of the occupied and oppressed states.

29. The political basis of imperialism is being steadily destroyed by self-determination and the consequent independence of nations. The incentives of glory and power will be greatly dimmed by the suffering that will come to imperialistic nations from this war. Moreover, the economic pressures to imperialism through foreign trade, exploitation and emigration of excess population can be ameliorated for the future. In any event, with victory in this war, imperialism will be at the lowest point in history, at least for a while.

With United Nations victory the only important peoples who will probably be left under other states will be the Polynesian Islands and largely unsettled areas of Africa, who will at their present state of political development lay little claim to self-government.

Africa may well be called the "Dark Continent" in view of the prevalent ignorance of its problems. There is urgent need for study of the varied and intricate questions which will demand answers after this war.

Africa could long be considered a sort of Atlantis so far as the affairs of other continents were concerned. But even during the present war, with the spread of hostilities and the staggering development of aviation all continents are brought into a new and closer relationship. There are within Africa's borders vast spaces adaptable to white settlement and vast resources of raw materials needed by the world. Without exaggerating the growth of our immediate interest in other parts of the world, it has become obvious that it behooves us as a matter of common prudence to study the problems we have hitherto neglected, with a view to averting the growth of future threats to peace.

It is not our task to judge the record of the colonizing powers. There is much that is both good and bad in that record. To some, the good far outweighs the evil: the establishment and maintenance of public order; abolition of the slave trade; the development of national resources; greater markets for native produce; better health conditions; the cessation of tribal wars with all their cruelties; and greater opportunities. And last, but by no means least, the spiritual, educational, and social benefits from the spread of the Christian religion.

There are grave liabilities as well—in the introduction of new intoxicating liquors, the spread of diseases not known before, the breaking down of old customs and taboos of ethical value, and the evils arising from organization and industrialization.

The true picture is to be found, if anywhere, in a composite of the good and bad.

The problems of Africa are further complicated by the

different degrees of civilization of its peoples. These problems are too complicated to be settled at the peace table. There will be neither the time nor the objectivity needed for the task.

30. Perhaps the course that offers the greatest hope of sound achievement would be for the United Nations to negotiate agreement, before the end of the war, as to principles, and leave details to be worked out by international commissions. But experience shows that if such commissions are to achieve anything substantial they must have a clear mandate. They cannot operate successfully on the basis of general declarations which each nation is free to interpret for itself.

31. It is worth considering whether some of these latter areas in particular should not be put under international government with equal access to all nations for immigration, trade, and development of natural resources. Particularly could their open spaces, with proper organization, be made a refugee settlement for the oppressed of every kind and as an outlet for immigration from overpopulated nations without harm to the interests of the native populations.

Militarism

We said in Chapter I:

Man is a combative animal. He loves contest. He hates easily. He is an egoistic animal, and in the mass becomes more egoistic. His beliefs in superiority are quickly transformed into arrogance. And that is one of the stimulants of aggression. The pomp and glory of war have an appeal to man. He loves adventure, and to great numbers of people war becomes a wholesale relief from the dull routines of life.

Common defense is an age-old instinct. It started with the defense of the family and spread to the tribe and finally to the nation. By reason of this need of defense, every nation must have some degree of military organization, even among the most peaceful peoples. The possession of armament however, no matter how necessary, breeds suspicion, fear, counterarmament, and hate.

And out of military organization there often comes a military caste. Its hope of renown lies in war, not in peace. And its voice in government is more often for settlement of grievances by war than by the processes of peace.

The militarism we describe is an aggressive force. It always makes for war.

But military organization can have two quite different spirits. The one defense, the other aggression.

Like individuals, some peoples are naturally pacific and some naturally aggressive. China has been outstandingly the most pacific of all nations. So pacific has she been that in 3,000 years she has been conquered and ruled by foreign dynasties in all but two comparatively short periods.

Moreover, there is in some races a definite aggressive warrior strain. It grows in an aggressive race to a glorification of war for war's sake. The "reinvigoration" of the race through war has long been preached in Germany, Italy, and Japan. The "warrior concept" is deeply rooted in Germany, particularly in Prussia. This may be because of the constant threat of invasion. On the other hand, it has been argued that the trouble with the Germans is that, unlike the French and the Britons, they were never conquered by the Romans and given the advantages of that form of education. Tacitus was eloquent on the subject of Germany nearly 2,000 years ago. The Order of Teutonic Knights carried their thirteenth-century ideas with fire and sword. Their ideas of an aggressive military caste have come down through the centuries, with periodic modernizations, through Frederick the Great to Bismarck, with his "blood and iron," to Hitler, with his "master race," his "guns instead of butter."

The same could be said of the Japanese. Their two feudal military clans—the Choshu and the Satsuma—are represented today in the control of the Army and Navy respectively.

Probably 80 per cent of the German and Japanese people are no more militaristic than any other. But by their very docility they are constantly overridden by the warrior groups.

And we must not overlook the Pied Pipers, consumed with ambition, who call their countrymen to glory and conquest. These men, seeking power on earth and a place in the eternity of history, are the apotheoses of militarism and aggression. They are the Alexander the Greats, the Ghengis Khans, the Julius Caesars, the Charlemagnes, the Gustavus Adolphuses, the Napoleons, the Kaiser Wilhelms, and the current exhibits [p. 15].

32. Our experience since 1919 points to some profound deductions confirmed by even earlier history. One of them is: Disarmament offers the only effective way to bring militarism under control.

The problem falls into two phases: the disarmament of the enemy countries, and the reduction of arms in the victorious countries.

It is not to be expected that the victorious countries, having defeated aggressive militarism at infinite cost, are going to melt their swords and allow the enemy to return to the practices of the last hundred years.

Therefore, the first part of the problem resolves itself into disarmament of the enemy; the second part is disarmament among the Allies.

DISARMING THE ENEMY. The first lesson that we may well draw is from the experience in disarming the enemy states in 1919. By the Armistice and the Treaty of Versailles, their arms were destroyed and their navies were surrendered. Germany was permitted to retain a professional army of 100,000 men, supposedly for purposes of maintaining internal order. She was permitted to have a navy severely limited in tonnage and types of ships.

We have pointed out earlier that the huge mistake was that it perpetuated her professional armies and navies. It perpetuated the warrior caste and all its traditions. It afforded a skeleton army and navy of skilled men ready for quick expansion. It insured the continuity of the German General Staff and all their military skill, brains, and ambitions.

Repeated experience with this warrior caste in its bluffs, intimidations, aggressions, blitzes, and attacks without even declaration of war should be enough for the world in this particular. We must make a better job of it this time.

33. The complete idealistic view would perhaps be the total dissolution of the military establishments of all enemy nations and the substitution, for purposes of a civic order, of a constabulary of the police type, excluding the whole officer and military caste from such organization and thus assuring their disappearance from the world.

That is, no doubt, too much to be hoped for in this world, but it will serve as an ideal toward which men can strive.

GENERAL DISARMAMENT. The Treaty of Versailles contained a pious pledge of all the Allies to disarm sometime but made no provision for when or how.

The opposition among the victorious nations was rooted partly in fears that security could be provided only with overwhelming armies and navies. It came in part from mutual distrust among the former Allies themselves. Military alliances sprang up at once. The essence of military alliance is large armed force, and alliances are at once a block to disarmament. The heightened nationalism which arose inevitably from the war also contributed to each country's desire for arms. Arms were made easily accessible to the liberated nations by extensive sales from the larger Allies on credit. And there was the grim fact that masses of professional soldiers had been created who wanted to hold their jobs. To some extent, war industries wished to continue their markets. This was particularly the case in France, where a vicious combination of arms manufacturers with press and banking connections deliberately cultivated war scares and pressures to promote sales at home and abroad. America was not free from this taint, as witness the transactions around the Naval Conference of 1927.

Human nature and national mores being what they are, all this will happen again unless positive measures are taken immediately while the world is sick of killing and wants action to end it. The opportunity for comprehensive action will be of short duration. Unless this opportunity is seized upon, all these same obstructions will grow again —nationalism, imperialism, military alliances—and the witches, fear, hate, and revenge will mix a new brew.

They all demand armies and oppose disarmament. Experience at the last peace showed that once the flame of war horrors had died down, forces quickly sprang up which destroyed all hope of real disarmament. It required but a short time for these oppositions to grow and mobilize.

34. Therefore, experience shows if there is to be a reduction of arms among the victorious nations, it must be agreed upon in advance and action should take place within weeks, not months or years, after the firing ceases.

The victorious nations will automatically demobilize a great part of their huge war establishments. But even after that was done following the last war, enormous peacetime establishments remained. The burden of them to the taxpayers and to national economy by separation of men from productive labor was a contributory cause to the general economic collapse. When this war is over economic necessities will cry even more loudly for relief from such burdens.

35. If the rate of $20,000,000,000 spent annually in the world on arms before this war could be reduced to small dimensions immediately with the end of the war, that alone would ensure the recovery of economic life and civilization. The people of Germany, Japan, and Italy would surely have every reason to welcome that relief.

To be realistic, we must conclude that some military establishment will be retained, at least by the United Nations. The problem falls into two stages: first, the minimum necessary to assure defense, and second, the comparative armament of other nations.

Before discussing the character of disarmament, we must digress to mention the great shift in war methods. The developments since the last war have had a profound effect, not alone on the whole method of this war, but also an enormous effect upon the problems of disarmament.

These changes in the main lie in the advance of air power. It has tended to make the offense of armies more powerful than the defense. Land armies without large air contingents are at a great disadvantage. At the same time, it has enormously strengthened defense against naval attack.

The whole question of the effectiveness and value of surface ships is now in doubt. Without accepting the view that capital ships are now wholly useless, it can be said that naval attack upon land defenses is now extremely difficult if not practically impossible against adequate land-based air power. Nevertheless, the question of naval arms to be retained will also be modified by the whole shift in the relation of aircraft to surface warships. The sinking or disabling of a large number of first-class battleships and a host of cruisers and lesser craft, from the air in this war, all accumulate at least to raise a grave question as to the future utility of large surface navies. And, therefore, naval disarmament becomes an easier dose for the Powers to swallow.

The naval situation with victory should also be still more simple than that after the last war. Germany, Italy, and Japan will, or should, lose their entire navies with defeat. The French, who proved so great a stumbling block in naval disarmament after the last war, are not likely to oppose effectively any United Nations program. The only consequential remaining naval powers will be the United States, Great Britain and Russia. But Russia did not have much of a navy at the beginning of this war, has lost much of what she had, and does not appear to have been engaged in substantial naval building during the present war. With victory, the substantial navies remaining will presumably be those of the United States and Britain.

There will, however, be the old question of relative naval strength as between the victorious nations. The huge naval strength maintained after the last war, as we have said, was not out of fear of the disarmed enemy, but out of fear of one another felt by the Allies. The whole painful negotiations of naval limitation of certain ratios are proof of all that. At least this problem will be much simplified by our being no longer compelled to compromise with the wishes of France, Italy and Japan—and having already established the principle of parity between the United States and Britain.

The preservation of order on the seas from pirates, and assistance in the preservation of order in semi-barbaric countries fronting the seas could be done with only a small fraction of the naval strength provided in the naval-limitation treaties of 1922 and 1930.

With victory, the problem of land disarmament will be further simplified at the end of this war as compared to the last war. The land and air forces of Germany, Italy, Japan, Rumania, Bulgaria could be disarmed as far as necessary by the armistice itself. Hitler has destroyed every army in Europe except those of Russia, Turkey, and Spain. The only consequential land armies after the armistice will be American, British, Chinese, and Russian.

The opportunity to disarm enemy countries to a reasonable degree, the lessening of the number of armed nations to be consulted, and this rise of air power open another avenue of thought on the whole question of reduction of armament.

36. The sole possessor or possessors of military air power could stop anyone from going to war. And international action to enforce peace would be enormously simplified.

There enters into this question an element arising from commercial air power. During this war, the design and effectiveness of war airplanes have shifted away from the design and effectiveness of commercial planes to a degree almost comparable with the divergence of types of warships and merchant ships. This divergence in design and equipment in the two categories of airships has gone so far that types of civilian planes probably no longer can be used for military purposes. The contrary is also true to a large extent. Therefore, it is possibly not necessary to limit commercial planes in order to secure air disarmament. Nevertheless, this question is not so definitive as not to require reservations. It calls for discussion and study.

There enters into this question of relative arms among nations an additional approach to the problem. As we have stated, in 1932, Mr. Hoover, through Mr. Gibson, chairman of the American delegation to the Disarmament Conference, proposed the abolition of all offensive arms —that is, bombing airplanes, submarines, large mobile guns, tanks, and poison gas. All but a few large nations agreed to it at that time—some forty-five of them. This proposal was revived and earnestly advocated by President Roosevelt in 1933. And battleships might now be included.

The effect would be to make the defense ascendant over the attack. While nations may violate such agreements to some extent secretly before the war or after war begins, yet it is impossible to make these instruments so quickly and in such large quantities as to be overpowering. Had that proposal for the abolition of aggressive arms been accepted and enforced as provided in the American proposals, the blitz would not have been possible.

37. In any event, victory will offer an unparalleled opportunity to disarm and thereby reduce the cost and dangers of arms to the world to the lowest ebb for a whole century—and that would contribute much to quick recovery and lasting peace. But if it is to be done, it must be done at once at the peace table, not postponed.

The Forces of Fear, Hate, and Revenge

In the first chapter we stated:

> Fear, hate, and revenge play a large part in the causes of war. . . . Fear of invasion, fear of starvation by blockade in war, fear of economic disadvantage; age-old hates from wrong, from rivalries, from oppression; yearnings for revenge for past wrongs and defeats—all press toward violence.
>
> These great forces of violence lie deep in the recesses of racial consciousness and racial experience. These emotions are the inheritance from all previous wars. Wrongs live for centuries in the minds of a people. There are traditional age-old hates between nations which are burned into their souls. From these emotions, wars have bred new wars. They have seldom settled anything. Fear of stronger races by their weaker neighbors born of invasions and defeat keeps them in constant sacrifice for the burdens of defense.
>
> It keeps them in constant agitation, seeking diplomatic action, seeking support and military alliances. And the humiliations and privations of defeat and punishment create an undying demand for revenge.
>
> The defeated are always humiliated. They are always impoverished. Either in reality or belief, the national pride, the national hopes, the national economy, or the national dignity of the vanquished have suffered. No nation ever recognizes or admits that it is wrong. No leader of that nation would dare suggest such a thing. Hate lives on, and it becomes entrenched in the mores of a people.
>
> These emotions are eternal inheritances and causes of war. They, too, will sit at every peace table [p. 19].

These total wars of the last generation are far greater breeders of hate than ancient wars. No longer is there chivalry of armed men for women, children, the aged and infirm. Starvation of nations has brought not only agony to civilians, but stunting of their children and decimation of millions from inevitable pestilence. Women and children have been killed in tens of thousands by bullets, fire, and bombs from the air. The hideous cruelties of blitz surprise, the sinking of seamen without compassion by submarines, the attacks upon helpless Jews, murder of hostages, the refusal of liberal governments to allow food to their conquered allies—all not only make a ghastly picture of barbarism, but they raise the emotions of peoples to heights of lasting fear and hate.

The whole experience of Versailles shows that these forces will not only sit at the peace table, but will influence international relations for generations unless there are statesmen far more elevated in spirit than sat at the last peacemaking.

Shrill cries for punishment will echo through every part of the peace deliberations. Yet we must realize that the mass of Axis peoples are no more responsible for starting this war than the last one. We must remember they have been under dictatorship, their people have been misled, wrongly educated, and were allowed to have no will in this war. They have been terrorized and deprived of the truth. But there is a large question of the personal responsibility of heads of state and their associates for violation of treaties and agreements, entered into with free will, in pursuit of militaristic and imperialistic designs which result in the killing of millions of human beings.

38. There is just one discrimination that can and should be made. The leaders of the nations who brought this situation upon the world must be made to realize the enormity of their acts. There can be no moral distinction and there should be no legal distinction between such men and common criminals conspiring to murder. Too long has it been assumed that there is something sacred about the heads of state who project or provoke war and wholesale murder.

It may well be borne in mind that defeat and disarmament of a nation is in itself the greatest humiliation that comes to a people. To continue punishment or to try to hold peoples in bondage is not only statesmanship terrible in its consequences, but is an illusion.

39. Nations cannot be held in chains. In the end there can be no trustworthy security except by giving the decent elements in a people a chance to co-operate in the work of peace.

REPARATIONS. The problem of indemnities and reparations will arise. Aside from the loss of life, the cost of the war to the victorious nations will be more than the whole national wealth of the Axis Powers. The debts alone of the United Nations will not be less than $500,000,000,000, and the continuing cost of pensions and interest will add other hundreds of billions. Therefore, there can be no real reparations. The first World War proved that no considerable sums could be collected in any event. The total payments of Germany on reparations were not much more than the money she borrowed from the Allies and subsequently repudiated. After this war, some minor sum might be had.

40. Defeated people simply will not produce to pay huge reparations. And they cannot be made to do so. If the peacemakers resolve to take a few billions over a few years to give as a bonus to their widows, orphans, and maimed, with a few articles of vertu *as mementos of the war, they will save much worry at the peace table.*

Further, debts from one Allied Power to another are valueless. With the doors of free speech and propaganda open, people will squirm out of them somehow. Moral justification will be found by every demagogue against payment. It will be an issue in every election.

41. The fact is that there cannot be any continuing intergovernmental debt of consequential amounts between governments in either reparations or loans.

We may go back to the peace made after the other two great crises in modern civilization for experience in this matter. Historians find that mankind had some surcease from world war after the Treaty of Westphalia in 1648, and after the Treaty of Vienna in 1815, but they can find no peace from the Treaty of Versailles in 1919.

The two previous great treaties avoided one error of the Treaty of Versailles. They did not try to punish the vanquished nations or put them into economic bondage. That may possibly explain the fact that they prevailed so much longer than the Treaty of Versailles.

42. Certainly, experience shows that no nation can be punished as a whole and at the same time leave any hope of lasting peace. This endless treadmill of punishment must be stopped in the world if there is to be real peace. Victory with vengeance is ultimate defeat in the modern world.

We can have peace or we can have revenge, but we cannot have both.

CHAPTER XIII

Methods of Preserving Peace

IN THE last three chapters we deduced some conclusions, from world experience, upon the foundations which must be laid for peace by allaying the destructive action of the six dynamic forces of ideologies, economic pressures, nationalism, imperialism, militarism and the complexes of fear, hate, and revenge. After these foundations are laid, a superstructure must be built where the seventh force, the will to peace, shall preside. Not only at Versailles, but time and again, it has been proved in the history of the world that unless these foundations are rightly built, no international co-operation for preservation of peace can be successful. But there must be such a structure. It is one of the great obligations upon the peacemakers.

The purpose of this chapter is not to advocate any particular form of such international action, but to present the different proposals objectively. World experience is more positive in the requirements of the foundations than in the architecture of the temple itself.

In describing the will to peace at the outset of this essay, we said:

> Against all the forces which make for war stands the will to peace. Ever in the background of men's minds is the infinite suffering of war. It kills or maims the best of the race. It brings the deepest of all griefs to every home. It brings poverty and moral degeneration. It brings these poignant ills to victor and vanquished alike.
>
> The Sermon on the Mount launched the transcendent concept of compassion, of peace and good will among men as a fundamental of the Christian faith. And despite all his violation of the spiritual concepts, man has received from them an undying inspiration to strive for peace.
>
> The search over centuries by men of good will for methods of lasting peace testifies to the yearning of peoples for relief from the world's greatest blight. The multitude of peace treaties, the establishment of embassies and legations, the Holy Alliance, the Concert of Europe, the balance of power, the development of international law, the Hague Tribunal, the processes of settlement of controversy by negotiation, by mediation, by arbitration, the League of Nations, and the World Court are all exhibits of the impelling will to peace.
>
> And indeed the spiritual concepts of peace have brought it to pass that every war must be justified by its leaders as a war of defense and for the purpose of securing peace. And the end of every war is received with joy and the ringing of the church bells [p. 20].

There are several methods for preserving peace which we believe should in a sense be added to the foundations of peace by incorporation into all the actual agreements directly between nations in addition to their operation by the instrumentality set up to preserve peace.

The peace treaty must necessarily make political, military, and economic settlements. It must provide some sort of international machinery or organization for preserving peace.

43. *But the step we here suggest is that there should be direct agreements between signatories which would tend to settle many controversies before they need reach any such international body. That is, each nation should agree to refer all disputes to arbitration or to refer them to judicial settlement or to establish cooling-off periods with independent investigation.*

Such direct treaties have been current between enlightened nations for many years and have served a great purpose. This suggestion is to make them universal, and thereby localize disputes and burden the international organization only in cases where these means of direct settlement of disputes should fail. Important in this category is the necessity to provide in the foundations of peace provision for adequate revision of onerous treaties.

Revision of Treaties

Certainly, experience shows that peace can best be preserved, not by preventing change and putting the future in a straitjacket, but by seeking to control change and direct it. Obviously, any attempt to maintain the *status quo* indefinitely is a direct invitation to war—for peaceful means being denied, the change can come only through force. War becomes the only available solvent. If provision is made that there will be revision of treaties by adequate orderly methods, it can be hoped such revision will be done peacefully.

44. *It is, therefore, suggested that the objective should be to build the concepts of revision into the body of international law to a place of equal importance with the*

other pacific methods, alongside of conciliation, mediation, arbitration, judicial decision, and cooling-off periods. It is further suggested that the application of any nation for revision of treaty provisions, not sooner than ten years after its conclusion, should be implemented by the appointment of a committee of outstanding statesmen not interested in the dispute to report and negotiate a reasonable settlement.

International Machinery to Preserve Peace

The preservation of peace, however, must finally rest upon some sort of co-operative international organization which will continuously allay and keep in check the vicious elements of the dynamic forces which make for war and will constantly strengthen those forces which make for peace.

History is probably less instructive on what to do in the future than it is on what not to do. Nevertheless, experience is the substance of reason and a better guide on what to do than is Utopian emotion. If we go back over all these centuries of mankind's contriving of machinery to preserve peace, we find they divide into two categories.

The first method, historically, is to maintain peace by force. The Pax Romana, the balance of power, military alliances and counteralliances have been used to make aggression at least more cautious. These methods may have served as a check upon war, but in the end they crashed by their inherent stimulation of militarism, nationalism, imperialism, fear, and hate. And as their processes involve many nations not direct parties to the conflict, they cause a wider spread of war. The League of Nations was by "collective action" to set up force differing from other forms in that it proposed the use of military or economic force by common action of all the other nations against aggressors.

The second category of peace preservations sprang from the growth of civilization itself, the very spiritual and moral basis of which lies in the control of the conduct of men by law and justice. After all, the preservation and advancement of civilization cannot be based on force. These processes, which we have called the pacific methods, are based upon the prevention of war by establishing respect for international law, fidelity to agreements, and settlement of controversies by pacific methods of negotiation, conciliation, arbitration, and judicial decision, and by agreement to abandon all war in favor of such pacific methods.

But rather than discuss the philosophy and methods of these two different ideas of peace preservation, we believe the reader will obtain a more direct approach to the problem if we take up the more important actual proposals that have been made for international action.

The plans for preserving peace, and which have been suggested, fall into eight major categories:

1. Restoration of the League of Nations under the Covenant as it stands.
2. Restoration of the League with a revised Covenant giving it absolute military power to enforce peace.
3. Restoration of the League of Nations with a revised Covenant constituting it as an effective Council of Nations to preserve peace solely by pacific settlements and for building international co-operation.
4. Proposals for a separate military organization by the leading allied nations to preserve order.

5. Proposals that each great region of the earth should separately organize its own preservation of order while co-operating in pacific settlement through some form of the League, Council of Nations, or other world organization for pacific settlements.
6. Extreme isolation.
7. Federation of nations.
8. Pax Americana.

We do not enumerate these possible courses in order of their importance—every student has a different view upon that. Some may prefer to mix the ideas into different forms.

These plans are in process of evolution. There are certain positive lessons from world experience with them which can be deduced. There are arguments for and against each of them. The best form cannot be determined until nearer the end of the war, when we have a clearer view of things to come and until there have been wide public consideration and debate. From such discussion will come better understanding of the problems. Without here expressing opinions of our own, we give the arguments, pro and con, and state such experience as the world has had with such methods.

1. RESTORATION OF THE LEAGUE OF NATIONS UNDER THE COVENANT AS IT STANDS. The League of Nations represents the greatest and most comprehensive experiment in all history in deliberate organization of nations to bring lasting peace. Indeed, we can grasp the value of this experiment only if we realize that the world has to learn its lessons in preservation of peace by trial and error.

The League failed to preserve peace. Yet it was by no means wholly a failure. We have sought to analyze fully its workings in Chapter VIII, to which we refer the reader for the background of these immediate observations.

There were many causes for this failure. Among them were the failure of the Treaty of Versailles to allay the six dynamic forces which make for war; the disastrous political climate arising out of the competition of power diplomacy, balance of power; military alliances which constantly ignored the League; the failure to support representative government in the enemy countries; and, finally, the economic miseries of Europe.

Despite these handicaps from outside, the League did succeed in developing a considerable measure of accomplishment in one field and an unparalleled measure of success in another. It did settle many controversies by pacific means; it did advance the technique of such settlements. Its outstanding success was in the development of co-operation between nations in the fields of public health, in advancement of welfare, in intellectual exchanges, and in economic improvement.

We have referred to the outside influences which militated against the success of the League. There were, however, weaknesses in the League itself. We have analyzed these weaknesses elsewhere, but we may condense them here.

1. The Covenant of the League was at the same time too elaborate, too precise, and not precise enough in its provisions. The text became a yoke under which nations chafed or became fearful concerning their sovereignty. The attempt to commit nations to certain

procedures and at the same time to give them each a veto power over action led to destructive effects. In consequence, there were incessant disputes over interpretation, jurisdiction, and authority.

2. The original theory of the League was that all controversies between nations should be submitted to pacific settlement and that if any nation refused and began military action, it was to be dealt with as an aggressor. Thereupon, collective economic or military force should be applied by the other members. This definition of an aggressor proved to have great difficulties. But more important, the compromises in the Covenant by which nations did not bind themselves to this procedure and with the provision of a full veto power to each member the original theory never had a chance.
3. The League was thus founded upon two different concepts, one organizing the preservation of peace by economic or military force; and the other, for the prevention of war by settlement of controversy through pacific methods. The two concepts clashed. In any event, the attempt to summon economic and military force against important aggressors proved beyond the practical capacity of an international body, and with these failures the strength and prestige of the League in the field of pacific settlements were fatally injured.
4. The League did not recognize, or was prevented from undertaking, one of the first functions of preserving peace: that is, the need for comprehensive consideration of the political forces in different areas which were developing strains and the formulation of long-view policies and action for their correction. Regional development of such policies in Europe and Asia comparable to the work of the Pan-American conferences

in the Western Hemisphere was a constant and urgent necessity.

5. The League failed to provide for or secure any reality in the revision of onerous treaties or those made from the heat of war which could not endure. Thus, it became the defender of the *status quo* and left to war the dissolution of such strains.

It seems improbable that the membership of the League could be voluntarily restored without considerable amendment to the Covenant. Even if nations were forced to join, they could obstruct and withdraw unless the whole Covenant were revised.

Two categories of amendments are proposed. The one would take the League fully into the field of military force, the other would take it wholly into the field of pacific settlements.

2. RESTORATION OF THE LEAGUE WITH A REVISION OF THE COVENANT GIVING IT ABSOLUTE MILITARY POWER TO ENFORCE PEACE. One proposal for revision of the Covenant is to preserve most of its present structure but with revision so as to give the League complete power by making arbitration or judicial determination compulsory in all disputes; making refusal the sole criterion of aggression; making the economic and military sanctions follow automatically upon military action of such an aggressor; doing away with the veto power of each nation; making League decisions by majority or two-thirds vote; and giving the League an international army, navy, and air force to enforce its decisions.

It is asserted that this would "put 'iron teeth' in the League" and would make peace impregnable. This method would assume that "aggression" can be defined in these terms, but the experience which we have discussed indicates that it is not this simple.

And such an armed force would necessarily have to be larger than any combination of other armies, navies, or air forces, all of which implies that the disarmament of all nations must be very thorough, or, alternatively, that the League force be a very large one.

These ideas were discussed at length and rejected at Versailles. They, of course, mean a wholesale surrender of national sovereignty. The refusal of nations to join or abide by the much milder provisions of the present League would seem to indicate that it would not have many voluntary members. It would, in fact, be a blind acceptance of super sovereignty which nations in practice would probably refuse to accept, or, if they were compelled to accept, they would not abide for long.

A further criticism is that a majority of nations would not necessarily represent a majority of population. And that a combination of small nations, even if a two-thirds vote were required, might use the machinery for aggression on the larger ones. A further objection is that such an army, navy, or air force would have to be commanded by human beings of some nationality, and they would not be likely to attack their own people; and conversely, they might on nationalist or other grounds be influenced to attack others. When such proposals were raised at Paris in 1918, they were rejected, partly because no considerable adherence could be expected, and partly because it was recognized that a group of nations or the commander in chief of such an army could become dictators of the world.

3. Restoration of the League of Nations with a Revised Covenant Constituting It as an Effective Council of Nations to Preserve Peace Solely by Pacific Settlements and for Building International Co-operation. Another proposal is made for amendment of the Covenant which takes account of the weaknesses of the present League idea and its structure and seeks to build up and strengthen it in the directions where it has proved to have been the most successful. The proposal amounts, in fact, to a transformation of the League into a continuously sitting Council of Nations—each nation to be permanently represented by the highest-caliber men of more than ambassadorial rank, with the purpose of the League confined to developing broad regional policies for peace; to bringing about settlement of controversies under existing treaties through negotiation, arbitration, and judicial settlement; and to promote revision of onerous treaties. The use of force would be divorced from its proceedings. The League is to be, it is suggested, a continuous round table of nations through direct representatives of chiefs of states and Ministers for Foreign Affairs.

This would also be a radical departure from the practice of the League, which was seldom to convene the nations until after a crisis had arisen.

Broadly, it is proposed to preserve the name and that the Covenant be revised:

1. To eliminate all clauses dealing with military and economic sanctions.
2. To eliminate all clauses presuming to commit nations to specific procedure in the settlement of disputes.
3. To substitute for these clauses the simple declaration

that it shall be the duty of the League to promote pacific settlements.

4. To substitute for the Council and Assembly as at present constituted a body composed of ambassadors from all nations, resident at all times at the seat of the League, with no binding votes except upon procedural questions.
5. To elect annually a President from its membership with an annually elected Executive Committee on procedure and organization.
6. The Executive Committee to appoint subcommittees from its membership upon a regional basis to formulate regional policies of peace. For Europe, for instance, it would be, in effect, a Concert of Europe constantly operating. Its President, upon such regional committee's failure to secure settlements, to have power to appoint a more general committee from members not parties to the dispute.
7. All committees simply to negotiate, conciliate, urge adoption of pacific methods, report on facts and recommend to the whole body, with no penalties or obligations.

In fact, the proposal seeks to get away from rigid organization to a constantly functioning clearinghouse and round table of international questions, where each nation is effectively and at all times present in the person of a leading personality acting in close collaboration with his own Foreign Office.

Fundamentally, this is a modernization of diplomacy. It would tend to hold the heads of states and their Foreign Ministers more directly in the picture of responsibility instead of in a stand-off attitude negotiating with a separate body, as the League was regarded. It is proposed that the League should preserve and encourage all the treaties of arbitration, all the machinery of the World Court and the Hague Tribunal—it being one of the purposes of the League to secure that controversies be referred to and solved by such agencies or special committees as the occasion might require.

The plan proposes that the admirable organization of the existing Secretariat be re-established with all of its excellent machinery of international co-operation under the direction of this reorganized League.

No machinery of enforcement is suggested. It would rest solely upon good faith, world opinion, and the value of immediate discussion directly between nations rather than through the intervention of an outside body.

Carrying no commitments or delegations of sovereignty, it is contended not a single voice in any country could object to full membership.

It is held that such a Council, out of experience and successful precedent, could be expected to build up the fabric of international law and steadily guide the movement of nations toward abolition of war.

One objection to this plan is that some organization of force methods to preserve peace will be necessary for some years to come, but the contentions of its advocates are that experience has demonstrated that the two functions of force and pacific settlement are incompatible and mutually destructive when exercised by the same organizations, and that ultimate hope must be in the growth of pacific methods. The proposers hold that force measures to preserve international order should be separately erected elsewhere, somewhat as described next.

4. Proposals for a Separate Military Organization by the Allied Nations to Preserve Order. The history of 140 years amply indicates that among the multitude of nations in Europe and Asia there must be some kind of military restraints if there is to be peace. The long catalogue of a hundred military alliances and interventions of the balance of power intended to prevent war is in itself ample proof of this.

After the Napoleonic wars the Quadruple Alliance performed this function during the readjustment period. After the first World War the military power of Britain, France, and Italy served after a fashion until their joint relationships began to disintegrate and the League failed with "collective security." The job was bigger in 1919 than in 1815 partly because of the multiplication of independent states.

The organization of economic, military, or other force action to preserve peace is, however, the most difficult problem that civilization has to confront. The world is today not only divided by its nationalisms, but it is also divided by militant ideological groups whose emotions and devotions to their ideas are not going to evaporate with peace.

One lesson the world should have learned by this time. That is that economic sanctions mean war when they are applied to a strong nation and therefore can be abandoned as a method of force more likely to make for war than peace.

The foundation of any police measures must first be laid in general disarmament. Technically, for reasons given elsewhere, this is simpler than hitherto. The possibility after general disarmament of stopping aggressive action by a comparatively small air force as distinguished from large armies and navies offers more arguable approach to the problem than hitherto.

Most students agree that it is a reasonable deduction from all history that after the present war, with its even larger number of states which "self-determination" will create, and the increasing hates from total war, there must again be some strong military supervision if Europe and Asia are to keep the peace, at least until the malignant forces in those areas have had time to abate and the constructive forces to dominate.

The proposal of those advocating the transformation of the League into a Council is that the Allied Powers must, after the peace, take on the burden of policing the world for some period after the war, but should act only after the League, reorganized as above, had exerted its full energies to keep the peace.

In any event, if the realistic experience of former world wars is any criterion, even without definite organization, the victorious powers will, with military means, jointly dominate the world for so long as their interests do not clash. They will need to do so at least during a period for political and economic recuperation.

5. PROPOSALS OF SEPARATE CONTINENTAL ORGANIZATIONS TO ENFORCE PEACE. These proposals are that each great area—the Western Hemisphere, Europe, and Asia—should be organized for its own preservation of order, but co-operating in world pacific settlements through the League formed into a council of nations or other organization of the world for pacific settlements.

The proposers of these plans have in mind the separate problems and interests of the three great areas—Europe, Asia, and the Western Hemisphere. And they contend that not only are they thus separated, but that universal world organization for more than pacific settlements, such as the Council form of the League, are bound to break down.

The Western Hemisphere for a century, down to 1937, pursued a broad policy of separation from the conflicts of the other continents, with the exception of the one period of 1917 to 1920. And this policy was successfully maintained even in times when the Old World was wholly dominated by aggressive military dictators. The Spanish-American War, far from being an intervention in Europe, was another step in this hemisphere separation, which would have been completed with the independence of the Philippines. The Monroe Doctrine and the United States Navy served to maintain the separation by protection of the other states from Old World aggression. And the foreign policies of the other American republics were largely determined by their ability to count on us for protection against Old World aggression.

During the whole of the last century, the United States and the other nations of the Western Hemisphere co-operated, and at times gave the lead in co-operation with nations in the other continents in building up the body of international law and the settlement of conflicts by conference and other pacific means. At least as contrasted with Europe, a large degree of peace without fear has been maintained in the New World. This is well indicated by the fact that over this last century and a half in wars among the twenty-one nations of the Western Hemisphere, not more than 500,000 men have been killed, whereas in twenty-one nations of Europe alone, probably more than 15,000,000 have been killed.

The broad arguments that are advanced to the Western Hemisphere for the readoption of separate organization for the future are:

1. That behind the two oceans the Western Hemisphere can, with moderate modern defense measures, be kept free from Old World encroachment.
2. That power politics and wars on the other continents are unending, and thus the Western Hemisphere would be eternally involved in the inevitable destruction resultant from these wars.
3. That in this hemisphere we have the unique advantage of a score of nations in a single block, with a high level of international conduct, a common purpose, and a growing sense of solidarity.
4. That it is within neither the knowledge nor the capacity of the people of the Western Hemisphere, so far removed from the actual problems of the other continents and so divergent in their ideals, to engage in foreign power politics.
5. That their form of government, with recurrent changes of administration, cannot have the continuity of foreign policies necessary.
6. That the American weight thrown into Old World balances serves to disturb rather than steady them.
7. That civilization in this hemisphere can make progress only if it is unhampered by the setbacks of recurrent wars with their tolls of death and impoverishment.
8. That, while a policy of hemispheric separation involves non-interference in European and Asiatic politics and wars, this in no way precludes our cooperation with all countries in pacific means for maintenance of peace.

9. That unless we refrain from taking part in the wars of Europe and Asia, far from saving civilization, we shall only contribute to its destruction everywhere.
10. That the Western Hemisphere has no self-imposed mission, responsibility, or strength to compel peace on the other continents.
11. That the Western Hemisphere already has its foundations of organization in the Pan American Union and conferences.
12. And that by keeping the lamp of liberty burning brightly in this hemisphere, there is a beacon and a sanctuary to the whole world.

The arguments against such a policy are:

1. That communication, transportation, and trade interdependence of the two hemispheres have narrowed our great ocean barriers so that former physical separation is greatly reduced.
2. That the military airplane has reduced the defensive value of the two oceans.
3. That advanced bases necessary for our protection bring us into European problems.
4. That the growth of aggressive centers within Europe and Asia threatens the Western Hemisphere's independence.
5. That the Western Hemisphere cannot suffer the engulfment of liberty-loving nations of Europe and Asia without lasting harm to itself.
6. That the spread of liberty throughout the world is a prime concern to this hemisphere, both in self-defense and spiritually.
7. That this is a responsibility which we cannot avoid.
8. And further, that having now departed from our tra-

ditional policies by entering foreign power politics and joining in this war, we have created lasting hates and economic issues which require us, for some time after victory at least, to continue our involvement in Old World politics in order to protect ourselves.

The proposers of these plans of continental separation, except for co-operation in pacific means, believe that each continent should set up its own police force or, alternatively, that the Allies in this war should do the policing, each in their own hemisphere.

It is interesting to observe that through the history of both the United States and Great Britain there are recurrent waves of determination to be dissociated from wars between other nations. The movement toward involvement is always a reluctant process. And with the end of each war, with its deep wounds and huge losses, comes an inevitable reaction toward separation and aloofness.

For 300 years, Britain has lived cheek by jowl with these problems through her nearness to European conflicts. After participating in long and costly wars, she always reverts to a period—usually a long period—of deliberate separation. It sometimes goes further as a consciously adopted national policy eulogized as "splendid isolation." This was amply evident in the Peace Ballot of 1934–35, and the vote of the Oxford Union, pledging that its members would not fight in foreign wars. But sooner or later the cycle begins again, until the pressures for war become too strong to be resisted.

In our own case, the first real departure from our traditional policy in 1917 to 1920 also led to the inevitable reaction in the growth of a strong determination to keep out of foreign wars forever after. This reaction is inherent in the whole consequences of war and can no doubt be expected again.

6. EXTREME ISOLATION. Isolation of the continental United States from all other nations has never been a policy of our Government. In strict logic, it means getting ourselves behind a Chinese Wall, trading and communicating gingerly over the top. It means no less than complete abandonment of the Monroe Doctrine.

The arguments in favor of such a policy are found in our fortunate geographic position, in our large measure of self-sufficiency, the lack of military dangers from our immediate neighbors—Canada and Mexico—and the ability to protect ourselves from serious invasion by any combination of nations from overseas.

The argument against this policy is the danger of overseas domination of Latin-America by European or Asiatic nations, and would require each Western Hemisphere nation to become an armed camp with all those dangers to liberty. Such a policy has never been tried and is more a descriptive term than a reality.

7. FEDERATION OF NATIONS. Another group of proposals for the maintenance of peace are those which advocate some form of federation between nations. There is a broad range of such plans.

The simplest envisages a Federal Union of the United States and the British Empire. Some expand to include all democracies. The most comprehensive of all urge world-wide federation, including all civilized states.

Most of the plans for federation have certain fundamentals in common, with variations in detail. They all provide for a supergovernment over the member nations to be conducted by representatives of the member states.

The proposals vary as to how the supergovernment should be composed and chosen. They rest usually upon extending the Bill of Rights and the general authorities of the American Constitution to the supergovernment. Some advocate that representation of the different nations should be based upon population, some on equal representation from each nation, some on a compromise by an upper house constituted like our Senate, and a house of representatives based on population. They vary in ideas as to where the seat of the supergovernment should be, but generally favor some neutral spot outside Europe and outside the United States.

It is usually proposed that citizens or subjects of any member state are to enjoy the privileges of citizenship within the boundaries of all other member states; that there is to be a common nationality. These plans usually provide for the maintenance of national governments subordinate to the supergovernment. But all questions of peace and war are to be vested in the supergovernment, which has full control of the armed forces of the member state and of its foreign relations. These plans also generally envisage the removal of all tariff and economic barriers, of the restrictions on immigration among the member states, and provide for a common currency and for other matters of common concern.

The more important plans limit the member states to the democratic nations or to those which may become democratic.

There are eight major arguments advanced in favor of federation:

1. That such a great military power would assure free-

dom from attack and could prevent the rest of the world from disturbing the peace.

2. That experience of the American Union shows that members of the supergovernment would stand to gain in the same way as did the states of the American Union through surrender of powers to the Federal Government.
3. That it would curb excessive economic nationalism and promote economic prosperity.
4. That non-democratic nations, impressed by the advantages of membership in the federation, would adopt democratic forms and methods and seek admittance—and thus increase the area of law-abiding nations.
5. That it satisfies the deep yearning to provide more sure survival of democracy and some escape of the world from its heartbreaking vicissitudes.
6. That if peace is to become the natural state of the world, we must outgrow the system of a community of separate states, each exercising full sovereignty, the right to make war, to create trade barriers and restrict immigration; that these and other rights must be surrendered to a central authority in return for greater security.
7. That a nation can no longer be final judge in its international controversies and that, as in the case of the individual, it must submit to the jurisdiction of recognized tribunals; that the use of force for self-defense is justifiable, but that the nation cannot be sole judge as to what constitutes self-defense.
8. That nations must recognize that the world has become an economic unit and forego the right to carry

on a separate economic policy within each watertight compartment.

A host of objections are raised from an American viewpoint, which comprise the following major ideas:

1. That, next to religious faith, the deepest of spiritual emotions are love of country and patriotism; that these emotions are embedded in struggles and sacrifices to maintain independence; that they embrace constructive ideals, unity of purpose, and symbols, all of which would be greatly injured or reduced in vitality by being melted into a foreign alloy; that their submergence in a new formation cannot be taken lightly.
2. That our nation has in 300 years grown apart from even the democratic ideals of other peoples. In some of them, class government still lingers; in others, democracy is little better than oligarchy.
3. That what relief we enjoy by the separation of two oceans from the age-old frictions and hates of Europe and Asia would be lost and their problems would be brought within our frontiers.
4. That several of the other democratic nations are burdened by the vast imperialistic problems of hundreds of millions of people of backward races, such as those of Africa, also of hundreds of millions of alien races, such as those of India and Malaya; and many of the democracies suggested for membership are themselves of different language and ideals and political development altogether.
5. That, being a minority in a supergovernment, the political, economic, and social control of our country would ultimately pass from our own hands, and all

the assurances of our fundamental institutions would be lost.

6. That this more distant authority in conducting our foreign relations, in making war and peace, and in military service takes such control further from the people.
7. That we have a host of unsolved economic, governmental, and social problems, the solution of which would be determined or influenced by majorities from these other nations, and as we have the major natural resources they would sooner or later be divided among others with great lowering of our own standards of living.
8. That we are a strong-enough country, if we do not go to sleep, to defend the Western Hemisphere from invasion by any aggressor, and that if we want military support, it can be had by military alliance.
9. That the economic shocks of the arrangement would be too great to bear in time of national impoverishment which must follow war.
10. That the setting up of such a federation on the basis of democratic ideology would, sooner or later, result in military counteralliances or in federations among nations of other ideologies, and thus reduce the world to groups of gigantic armed camps.

It is also advanced that American opinion alone does not suffice to bring about such a federation. It must be desired by others. Under some of these plans, it is proposed that the component parts of the British Commonwealth would have independent membership in the supergovernment. This would seem to require more thought, as it would mean no less than dissolution of the Empire by transference of their loyalties to the supergovernment just as would be the case if the forty-eight American states were given direct membership.

From the British side, Viscount Cecil, one of the most confirmed of internationalists, in a careful analysis[1] strongly opposes the whole federation idea as entirely unsuitable for the British Empire.

8. PAX AMERICANA. The various proposals for some sort of military mentor for the world in the words of some of our spokesmen range into the idea "America must police the world for a hundred years" or "American democracy must rule the world"—a sort of Pax Americana.

The inevitable end of this latter idea, realized or unrealized by its advocates, is a sort of imperial America, establishing garrisons over the world and undertaking to direct the conduct of foreign nations. Those who think in this direction contend:

1. That it is the American destiny to rule the world with a new and more humane form of domination.
2. That traditional peacemaking and building up of the will to peace have proven a failure, and are outmoded.
3. That the world requires a wholly new order of peacemaking.
4. That America would do it all idealistically and for the good of the people concerned and of lasting peace.
5. That the British Empire and her stabilizing influence is passing and that some nation must dominate if the world is to have peace.
6. That America could, by directing development of the

[1]*A Great Experiment,* Oxford University Press, 1941.

world, so increase its wealth as to repay our great costs of the war.

There are a number of objections raised by those opposed to these ideas:

1. That it is the same "master race" ideology that pervades Germany, Japan, and Italy.
2. That it violates our pledges of "self-government" and "self-determination."
3. That it would mean that the New Rome would be at perpetual war.
4. That nations, though disarmed and helpless before tanks and planes, still value their independence to the roots of their racial souls; they would find a thousand ways of resistance to what in their minds would be subjection and oppression.
5. That such a system applied to civilized races would ultimately bring about a combination of all the world against America—and there are 2,000,000,000 people against 130,000,000 Americans.
6. That history repeats and repeats that the role of Imperator over civilized nations (no matter under what name) inevitably devitalizes the governing people and revitalizes the subjected nations.
7. That our people would be divided over the idea of such tremendous responsibilities and would be divided about the conduct of every enterprise.
8. That if America remains a representative democracy, and with changing government every four years, the electorate would probably shed these responsibilities somewhere along the line even if the task were otherwise possible.
9. That no government of personal liberty and repre-

> sentative structure can survive in the United States if we undertake the imperial role.

In these plans, the two hundred years of peace held by military domination under the Pax Romana are sometimes recalled. There is, however, a certain difference in the two situations. The Romans were, for the most part, engaged in imposing peace and civilization upon barbaric peoples. To apply it to civilized peoples is a different job. And certainly, representative government withered in Rome under this regime.

CHAPTER XIV

The Method of Negotiating Lasting Peace

FROM WORLD EXPERIENCE it is not difficult to predict the situation that will exist in the liberated and enemy areas immediately after the United Nations armies are victorious.

Our pledges in the Atlantic Charter of "self-determination" and "restored sovereignty" will countenance and encourage the creation of even more independent nations than at the end of the last war. These twenty-five or more liberated peoples in Europe and Asia will at once set up their own governments. They will no doubt call their representative assemblies into session to deal with their emergencies. They will immediately create some military force to maintain order and to hold the boundaries which they think are justly theirs. They will appoint diplomatic agents to support their claims in the peace settlements. Their industries will be damaged or ruined. Their ports, railways, and canals will be demoralized. They will seize all the rolling stock and canal boats they can secure to assure transportation to their people. They will all be short of food or actually starving. There will be devastating unemployment. They will be without credit or raw materials. Their long and terrible suffering will express itself in hate and violence toward enemy countries.

In the enemy countries, with defeat, leaders and government will be overthrown. Revolution will march and new men will come into ascendancy among whom there will be great ideological and political differences. These governments will have no credit; their industries will be paralyzed; unemployment will be general. The machinery for distributing and rationing what food they may still possess will break down, and, like the liberated nations, they also will be starving.

Therefore we cannot assume that the building of orderly government and the resumption of peace, industry, and production will proceed easily and smoothly in any of the war-ravaged areas. This time, as in the last, they will be retarded or undone by disorders, uprisings, wars, and passions.

45. From our examination of world experience in peacemaking, we believe it has been demonstrated that after world wars peace cannot be made adequately by such assemblies of scores of statesmen and diplomats as were convened at Vienna and Versailles.

The dynamic forces in many ways reach their most destructive point immediately after the cessation of hostilities. There are clamorous economic pressures for haste, that industry and trade may be resumed. There are the pull and haul of interests, the intrigues of nationalism and imperialism, the dangers arising from the white heat of fear, hate, and revenge, and the infinite complication of negotiation among a multitude of representatives of nations with divergent interests. All this tends to destroy and debilitate constructive effort and to drive toward improvised solutions, destructive compromise, and disregard of the fundamental forces in motion. Thus, the peacemakers are at the most disadvantageous moment to do their work.

General conferences of this character must consume time, and while debate and negotiation are in progress the whole world wallows in uncertainty, economic paralysis, political stagnation, and moral degeneration.

These past experiences show clearly the desirability of making peace under more favorable conditions, of giving time for destructive forces to abate and gaining time for reflection and negotiation in solving long-range problems.

46. We suggest that there should be a new and different approach to the whole machinery of peacemaking. We suggest that the peacemaking be divided into three stages:

(1) That instead of the usual military "armistice" with its deferment of peace, there should be substituted a "conditional" peace which would include not only the usual armistice provisions for ending combat but also the settlement of certain urgent problems which would reconstitute the forces of peace.

(2) An intermediate period—a breathing spell—for the rebuilding of political life and economic recovery.

(3) A further period for settlement of the long-view problems which require a cooling off of emotions. Without such a period we cannot hope for deliberation and careful development.

Such a "quick" and "conditional" peace as we suggest would take no more time to impose than the usual military armistice. In fact, it could be imposed by the military authorities on the battlefield, if the United Nations were agreed and prepared in advance. It would result in much quicker restoration of political institutions, public order, and economic life, all of which, as we have said, are weakened by the usual unsettling armistice followed by long and difficult negotiations.

47. Therefore, regardless of the character of the settlements to be made, we are convinced that there is one essential preliminary to any peacemaking; that is, before the end of hostilities there should be clear and unequivocal agreement between the victorious powers not only as to peace aims but also as to the methods to govern the peacemaking.

Such a "conditional" peace should include:

1. The instant surrender of arms and demobilization of all enemy military forces.
2. Repatriation of military prisoners and civil populations who have been driven from their homes.
3. The removal of all blockade measures against neutrals and liberated nations—and the removal of blockade against enemy areas the instant they have surrendered their arms and demobilized their forces.
4. Temporary restoration of pre-war commercial treaties pending general economic solution.
5. The designation of provisional boundaries of all states, liberated and enemy.
6. The immediate call of freely chosen elective constitutional assemblies or parliamentary bodies.

7. Immediate reduction of the armaments of the United Nations themselves to the minimum forces needed to maintain international order and to enforce ultimate peace provisions.
8. Acceptance by all liberated and enemy states of such future determinations as may affect these conditional arrangements.
9. Agreements by the liberated and enemy states to accept the machinery for the preservation of peace when it is settled.

Instead of a general peace conference of all these scores of nations the United Nations should create a number of separate international commissions to deal with such revisions of conditional arrangements as may be found necessary and with long-view problems such as the following:

1. The building of international machinery to preserve peace.
2. The definitive boundaries of liberated and enemy states.
3. The formulation of measures for the protection of racial minorities and provision for the transfer and resettlement of the populations in the irridentas where such solution is imposed by conditions.
4. The settlement of private property questions, damages from war, the return of plunder, compensations in machinery, plant, animals, etc., that have been ravished, including materials with which to rebuild destroyed areas.
5. Study of the various intricate problems of Africa with a view to agreement upon an enlightened course for the protection and development of the native

population; the use of sparsely settled regions to relieve the pressures of European populations and the development of natural resources for the benefit of the world as a whole.

6. The settlement of intergovernmental debts.
7. The settlement of long-view economic questions of international trade which affect lasting peace.

These conclusions can be far better arrived at after political and economic life has had a chance to recuperate and destructive emotions have been given time to cool off. Thus such assemblies as Versailles, with all its surroundings of false pomp, emotion, propaganda, high-pressure groups, and log-rolling governments can be avoided.

With victory and even a minimum of armed force in the hands of the victors alone, there need be no doubt of their ability to secure adherence to these conclusions.

48. We believe that during the interregnum period required for the growth of political order, economic recovery, the solution of these long-view problems, and the setting up of machinery to preserve peace, the victorious powers must:

(*a*) *Assure order in the world by military force.*

(*b*) *Instantly provide credits for food and its transportation in order to stay famine and pestilence. Otherwise there will be stunted minds and bodies, decimating death and anarchy upon which no lasting peace can be builded.*

(*c*) *Provide at once credits and raw materials in aid to the restoration of industry and employment and to enable the prostrate peoples to pay for their food supplies.*

The cost of these last two provisions will be much less with a quick conditional peace than with a demoralizing armistice, for they would allow the national credit to revive and production and exports to begin, and would lessen the demands upon the generosity of the few remaining strong nations.

49. The purpose of this war, the most terrible of three centuries, is to make a lasting peace. We must first win the war. But we will not win lasting peace unless we prepare for it. And we can prepare only by full and free public discussion and the cold surgery of analysis.

The historian can discuss the growth of the impelling forces, good and bad, which preceded the first two great convulsions in Western civilization when world-wide wars ended for a while in the peace treaties of 1648 and 1815. He can evaluate the relative weights of the forces which moved in those times, but we are still in the midst of this third explosion. It may be that the era of growing human freedom and economic materialism which began four hundred years ago with the Renaissance and has continued down to the present explosion is now in a crisis of change which will bring other concepts of civilization.

50. We have pointed out that if we scan these former convulsions of the modern Western world we can see that, following these long periods of general war and disorder, new shapes of civilization and new forms of nations have emerged. Civilization has taken new impulses and new directions. We must expect new forms and new directions from the gigantic explosion that began in 1914. No one can pretend to see these shapes clearly.

We know, however, that whatever forms evolve, the

seven dynamic forces will have a part in their shaping. And even if we are emerging into another era of civilization, then also we shall need peace. And this time the foundations of peace must be so laid that destructive forces are allayed, or again the structures that we erect to preserve peace will fail.

In the making of that peace will come a fleeting chance for leaders of mankind to bind the wounds, to restore faith, and to bring new hope to the world.

In the words of Washington to the Federal Convention:

> Let us raise a standard to which the wise and the honest can repair—the event is in the hand of God.

Appendix

FOR CONVENIENCE in reference, the authors have sought to tabulate the major and minor successes and failures of the League of Nations. The events of twenty years of League activity do not always lend themselves to hard and fast classification.

In the field of prevention of war, for instance, some sixty disputes were brought before the League. Some were delegated to the League for settlement by the peace treaties, some were submitted by member states, and some were passed along by the Council of Ambassadors. They differed widely in character and importance and in many of them it is difficult to determine the exact extent and effect of League action.

In some cases, it is true, war was stopped after fighting had begun (Yugoslavia and Albania, 1921; Greece and Bulgaria, 1925; Turkey and Iraq, 1924–26; Colombia and Peru, 1932). In some cases we find both success and failure. This is clear in the case of Vilna, where the League succeeded in stopping hostilities, but over a long period failed to end the quarrel and re-establish relations between Lithuania and Poland. In still other cases, disputes languished and died with no public evidence of effective League action; but there was sometimes a feeling that abstention from action had served a useful purpose and permitted controversy to die down without loss of face for either side. This will suffice to show the difficulties of hard and fast classification.

In addition to the settlement of wars and the preservation of peace, the League had large areas of success and failure in the field of non-political activity—a wide range embracing such different subjects as disarmament, financial reconstruction, the movement and protection of refugees, and health and social questions. These are perhaps even more difficult to classify. The following lists are therefore limited to League efforts to prevent wars and preserve peace and are offered as no more than an approximate outline of League activities in that field. Each reader remains free to make his own classifications and evaluations.

1. Major Successes

Mosul dispute, 1924–26. An admirable example of League activity. Dispute between Turkey (not a member of the League) and Great Britain (representing Iraq). The Council succeeded in stopping the fighting and securing the withdrawal of Turkish troops, which had crossed the frontier. Provisional frontier was drawn. Commission of Inquiry sent. Permanent Court consulted. After informal negotiation with both parties, the League solution was embodied in Treaty of Ankara, 1926.

2. Major Failures

Italian-Greek dispute—Occupation of Corfu, 1923. Italians murdered while fixing frontier line between Greece and Albania on behalf of Council of Ambassadors. Italy sent ultimatum and bombarded and occupied Corfu. Greece appealed to League. Italy rejected Council's proposal of arbitration, but accepted mediation by Council of Ambassadors. For fear of disrupting the League, the Council dealt gingerly with Italy and limited its show of authority to Greece, which was made to take the blame and pay damages.

China-Japan, 1931–33. Friction between the Chinese authorities in Manchuria and a Japanese garrison guarding the railway ended in Japanese attack and the seizure of several towns (1931). China appealed to the League. While the League was endeavoring to find a solution, Japan occupied the whole of Manchuria and set up the puppet government of Manchukuo, invaded Shanghai, and occupied various other points. Japan refused all offers of pacific solution and, on being designated and condemned as the aggressor by a resolution of the Assembly, withdrew from the League.

Italy-Ethiopia, 1935–36. A frontier incident at Walwal in late 1934 led to Italian demands of reparation. Ethiopia appealed to the League. Italy acquiesced in negotiation while preparing for war, counting on differences among the great Powers. Italy opened hostilities and, despite the application of sanctions, persisted until victory.

3. Minor Successes

Åland Island settlement, 1920–21. Conflicting claims of Finland and Sweden, settled by acceptance of solution proposed by League commissions.

Polish-Lithuanian dispute, 1920. League succeeded in preventing spread of armed conflict when Vilna was seized by the Poles in 1920.

Albanian-Yugoslav War, 1921–24. Under Council threat of economic blockade, fighting was stopped. The League followed up this action with various reconstruction activities, health organization, and famine relief.

Jaworzno, 1923–24. Frontier dispute between Poland and Czechoslovakia. Council, with advice of Permanent Court of International Justice, produced solution accepted by both sides.

Salgótarjan frontier dispute between Hungary and Czechoslovakia, 1923.

Burgenland frontier dispute between Hungary and Austria, 1923.

4. Minor Failures

Polish-Lithuanian dispute, 1920. Although the League was successful in preventing the spread of war, it failed in its efforts to reconcile the two nations and bring the quarrel to an end.

Eastern Karelia, 1921–22. Dispute between Finland and Soviet Russia over terms of Dorpat Treaty. League failure inevitable as Soviet Government refused to co-operate in seeking advice of Permanent Court.

Mur territory boundary dispute between Yugoslavia and Hungary, 1923.

Chaco dispute, between Paraguay and Bolivia, 1928, 1936. League efforts at conciliation and embargo of arms proved unsuccessful, and Paraguay finally withdrew from the League. Later settled by Conference of American States at Buenos Aires (1936).

5. Peacemaking Actions Outside the League Involving Several European Powers

April 1920. The San Remo Conference of Allied Powers dealt with various questions, one of which was a request of Germany for revision of part of the treaty, which was refused. Decided to leave settlement of the Fiume question to Italy and Yugoslavia.

June 1920. Hythe and Boulogne Conference of Allied Powers on Near Eastern questions.

November 1920. Treaty between Italy and Yugoslavia altering the Versailles Treaty setup of Dalmatian Islands.

May 1922. Genoa Conference of Allied Powers over Russia failed of agreement by French opposition.

November 1922. Washington Arms and Far Eastern Conference of nine Powers.

November 1923. Lausanne Peace Conference between Greece and Turkey which proved abortive.

July 1923. Second Lausanne Peace Conference. Principal Powers made peace between Turkey and Greece.

October 1925. Locarno Conferences of Britain, France, Germany, and Italy settled various questions.

June 1927. Naval Conference of United States, Great Britain, and Japan at Geneva.

August 1928. The Kellogg-Briand Pact signed.

February 1929. Agreement signed at Moscow by Russia, Poland, Rumania, Estonia, and Latvia, renouncing war.

January 1930. London Naval Conference: United States, Great Britain, France, Italy, and Japan.

July 1931. European nations agree to President Hoover's moratorium proposal on all intergovernmental debts.

August 1931. Principal Powers agree to President Hoover's proposal of a standstill agreement on all German private international obligations.

October 1932. Four Power Pact between England, France, Germany, and Italy.

July 1933. World Economic Conference was assembled at London upon the original proposal of President Hoover to deal with currency stabilization and trade barriers, but blocked by President Roosevelt's repudiation of it in a message to the Conference.

January 1937. British-Italian agreement on interests in the Mediterranean and Spanish affairs.

April 1937. Britain's recognition of Italy's sovereignty over Ethiopia.

September 1938. An agreement signed between Germany, France, Britain, and Italy at Munich, assenting to German occupation of Sudetenland.

6. Military Alliances or Non-Aggression Pacts or Mutual Guarantees of Frontiers Made outside the League

June 1919. Defense treaties between Britain, France, and the United States. (The United States did not ratify.)

August 1920. Military alliance between Czechoslovakia and Yugoslavia, subsequently including Rumania—The "Little Entente." Promoted by France.

February 1921. Military alliance between Poland and France.

March 1921. Offensive and defensive treaty between Poland and Rumania.

March 1922. Military alliance between Poland and the Baltic states.

April 1922. An alliance between Germany and Russia, agreed at Rapallo.

January 1924. French-Czechoslovakia military alliance.

October 1925. Renewed military alliances between France and Czechoslovakia, and France and Poland.

December 1925. Turkish Alliance with Russia.

April 1926. Treaty of "mutual security" between Iran, Turkey, Afghanistan.

November 1927. Treaty of friendship between Yugoslavia and France.

July 1933. A non-aggression pact between Rumania and Russia.

January 1934. German-Polish agreement of non-aggression (which marked practical abandonment of previous alliance with France).

February 1934. The Balkan pact, mutually guaranteeing frontiers between Turkey, Greece, Rumania, and Yugoslavia. It was, in fact, a limited military alliance.

March 1934. The Rome Protocols, organizing a Fascist Bloc of Italy, Austria, and Hungary, as opposed to the "Little Entente."

June 1934. Agreement by Rumania, Poland, and Russia, guaranteeing mutual frontiers.

September 1934. Military alliance for defense among Baltic states.

January 1935. Franco-Italian agreement settling African interests and co-operation in case of action by Germany.

April 1935. Stresa Conference of Britain, France, and Italy, establishing common front in view of German action in denouncing the disarmament clauses in the Treaty of Versailles the previous month.

May 1935. A military alliance between France and Russia.

May 1935. A treaty of mutual military assistance between Russia and Czechoslovakia.

June 1935. Britain signed a separate naval agreement with Germany, relaxing the Versailles provisions. France protested vigorously.

October 1936. Belgium denounced military alliance with France made during the war, and the German government guaranteed inviolability of Belgium.

October 1936. German-Italian military alliance—"The Axis."

November 1936. German, Japanese, Italian Anti-Comintern Pact. Japan practically joined the Axis.

March 1937. Treaty of non-aggression and mutual guarantees by Yugoslavia and Italy.

July 1937. Non-aggression Pact between Turkey, Iraq, Iran, and Afghanistan.

September 1937. Nyon Conference of nine Powers, establishing patrol zones around Spain.

December 1937. Germany and France entered into mutual guarantees of their frontiers.

November 1937. Poland and Russia renewed their non-aggression pact.

March 1939. Britain and Poland entered into agreement for mutual assistance.

April 1939. Spain joined Axis and signed the Anti-Comintern Pact.

April 1939. The Franco-British pledge extended to Rumania and Greece.

May 1939. Denmark, Estonia, and Latvia signed non-aggression pact with Germany.

May 1939. British-French-Turkish mutual assistance pact.

August 1939. Germany and Russia signed a non-aggression pact.

7. Violent Actions During the Life of the League

On the following acts of violence the League took no action.

April 1920. War between Poland and Russia.

June 1920. The Greeks made war on Turkey.

October 1920. Vilna seized in *coup d'état* by General Zeligowski.

October 1921. The Turks made war on the Armenian Republic and annexed it.

March 1921. The French army occupied certain German cities.

March 1922. A *coup d'état* overthrew the independent government of Fiume and annexed it to Italy. Armed rising in Upper Silesia under Polish Commissioner Korfanty to seize territory in spite of plebiscite.

January 1923. French and Belgians invaded the Ruhr. The British refused to take part.

January 1933. Italy shipped arms to Hungary despite disarmament treaties.

March 1935. Germany denounced the disarmament clauses of the Versailles Treaty.

March 1936. Germany reoccupied the Rhineland in violation of the treaties of Versailles and Locarno.

July 1936. In Spain, Germany and Italy give military aid to Franco. France and Russia to the Republican Government. France arranged a treaty of non-intervention which was freely violated.

March 1938. Germany annexed Austria.

October 1938. Poland seized certain provinces from Czechoslovakia.

March 1939. Polish ultimatum to Lithuania.

January–March 1939. Hungary invaded and annexed Carpatho-Ukraine.

March 1939. Germany annexed Czechoslovakia.

March 1939. Hitler annexed Memel.

April 1939. Italy invaded and annexed Albania.

September 1939. Germany attacked Poland.

September 1939. Britain and France declared war on Germany.

Index

Index

Index

Index

Index

Index